I0441850

DWAMENA EMMANUEL

Simple,

yet

GREAT

Getting your world to love simplicity
embedded with greatness.

Thank you *for*

reading this 21st Century Book.

Copyright © 2019 by **Dwamena Emmanuel**

Leading Books supports copyright. Copyright fuels creativity, encourages diverse voices, promotes free speech, and creates a vibrant culture. Thank you for buying an authorized edition of this book and for complying with copyright laws by not reproducing, scanning, or distributing any part of it in any form without permission. You are supporting writers and allowing Leading Books to continue to publish books for every reader.

First Published in Ghana.

Limit of Liability/Disclaimer of Warranty: While the publisher and author have used their best efforts in preparing this book, they make no representations or warranties with respect to the accuracy or completeness of the contents of this book and specifically disclaim any implied warranties of merchantability or fitness for a particular purpose. No warranty may be created or extended by sales representatives or written sales materials. The advice and strategies contained herein may not be suitable for your situation. You should consult with a professional where appropriate. Neither the publisher nor author shall be liable for any loss of profit or any other commercial damages, including but not limited to special, incidental, consequential, or other damages.

Part-title illustrations by Emmer Mena

All photos, unless indicated otherwise, are by Emmer Mena

Print Version ISBN: 13 – 9781072303824

9 7 8 1 0 7 2 3 0 3 8 2 4

Imprint: Independently published

Book design by Emmer Mena, adapted for eBook/Print

Cover design: Emmer Mena

Cover photograph: Emmer Mena

All rights reserved.

Version_1 - 2019

Dedication

I would like to thank God, my family. I dedicate this book to my future sons and daughters and my friends for their support, while writing this book. A special thanks to my friend, **Anita**, for her role in helping this book take shape. Last but not least, I want to show gratitude to all of my readers globally by saying "*Hello* "

Thank you...Thank you.... Thank you....

I love you all. We are One.

This page is intentionally left blank

Contents

Introduction

HOLY CRAP, I WROTE A BOOK! #Credit to

Lily Singh self-edited. Excerpt from How to be a Bawse: **#** Wait. Let me back up here. Hi! My name is **Emma**...and **HOLY CRAP**, I wrote a book! If you're reading this, I'm assuming it's for one of THREE reasons:

1. YOU ARE FAMILIAR WITH MY AMAZON / SOCIAL MEDIA PAGES / OR PERSONALLY OR GOOGLED, if so, thanks for supporting me outside of the digital space and allowing me to come through your screen and into your home like that terrifying GUY from *The Game of Thrones*.

2. YOU'RE A PARENT AND FOUND THIS in your child's bedroom and you're curious. You're also nosy and want to ensure that this book isn't filled with filth that will corrupt your Child's brain. Hi there! I can assure you that this book is family-friendly with a healthy hint of sass. My goal is to inspire your child to work hard and achieve great things. You should definitely buy three more copies and plant them around the house.

3. YOU HAVE NO IDEA WHO I AM or you've vaguely heard of me. That's completely fine. Maybe you're a total stranger who just wants to know how to live a simple yet great life, or maybe you are looking to add some diversity into your life. Mm mm...get ready for the ahaa! Moments.

This book is primarily my first and I intend to leave a valuable imprint on your heart even after my death. I believe *Simple, Yet Great* will not only accelerate the pace of growth of your facets of your life and business but will ignite you to another realm of futuristic possibilities you never dreamt were there. I have made it my mantra to live a simple life embedded with greatness. With that said, If I can do it, then you can do it even BETTER.

I therefore encourage you to join me on the journey of LEAVING A HALLMARK OR DENT IN THE UNIVERSE before we all pass onto the next life. Nothing is so enriching to have people tell you that through your talks, writings, supports, discoveries or inventions, and business changed their life.

Not only will you be remembered affectionately but forever will you remain in their lives. BE THAT PERSON who lives a Simple yet Great Life. Love you with all my heart.

LET'S KEEP THE INTRO SIMPLE...

Have you ever seen anyone on the street, and you thought, Arrrgh!! this guy seems to be looking good, but hey, it's going nowhere. Do you know why the persons thinks or reacts that way?
That person sees bulkiness and so much pride on the person that the victim doesn't even see.

This happens because our egos become our blind spots. We avoid simplicities thinking that taking on more would make us SUPERMAN...., I am here to provoke your thinking. With the advent of high-speed information transmission and the advent of technology, it has made our lives super easy and we are almost bellied with instant gratification everywhere we go.

The amazingly PERSONALITIES in this world whom many of us admire including me are just Super Simple – Great COMPANIES or BUSINESSES in this ERA are built, because they understand and implement subtle foundational policies or ideas to fasten the growth of their firm on OKR's(Objective Key Results), Key Performance Indicators(KPI) etc, simplified so that Customers will find their Products easy to use and affordable – giving a great experience moreover scaling up with speed.

Human beings seem to OPERATE at their best if they keep things super simple and adhere to it without compromise. It's purely nature's way.

Talk about finance
Talk about facets of business
Talk about Life ⟶ **Keep it Super Simple {K.I.S.S.}**
Talk about career
Talk about Relationships

Align your Ethics, Values and Philosophies with these and watch the world fall on you.

Join me through this book as I unleash the potent powers of living a Simple, yet great life in your life, family, career, businesses and relationships.

Getting the Best from This Book

1.<u>LIKE MOST RULES, EVERY RULE IN THIS BOOK</u> has an exception. In fact, don't even think of these chapters as rules; think of them as guidelines. Don't look for the unique scenario that disproves my point. In other words, don't be that annoying person in the YouTube comments section who has to be a Debbie Downer. If I say **"SMILE!"** don't yell, "But what if someone got paralyzed in a bungee-jumping accident and fractured their jaw and doesn't have the ability to smile anymore, Emma?" Don't focus on finding the loopholes but instead use that energy and focus on what you can learn. Also, if you got into a bungee-jumping accident and only fractured your jaw, you have a lot to smile about!

2.<u>BEFORE YOU READ THIS BOOK, I NEED YOU</u> to lay down your defense mechanisms. Take them off and put them away. I'm going to call you out and tell you you're slacking. I'm going to shine a spotlight on issues that make you uncomfortable and that you want to avoid. There's no room for excuses, justifications, or pity parties. Read the chapters with an open mind and resist the urge to get offended or defensive.

3. <u>THIS BOOK HAS A LOT OF INFORMATION IN IT</u>. I know that because it took me fifty years (an estimation) to write. Don't feel bad if you forget things! In fact, I encourage you to read chapters over and over again because living a simple yet great life is a process that doesn't happen overnight. Take notes. Rip out pages and plaster them to your wall. Do whatever you need to do to retain these guidelines.

4. <u>IN A LOT OF THE CHAPTERS,</u> I talk about how I apply each simplicity to my life. If you can't relate to these specific scenarios, that's completely fine and understandable. The goal is to understand the general principle and adapt it to your situation. I'm providing you with a framework—it's up to you to tweak it.

5. <u>DON'T GET MAD</u> at yourself or feel discouraged. This book is an opportunity to call yourself out, grow, make mistakes, and become better. Reading this book should be viewed as a journey

toward something positive, not an exercise in judgment and criticism.

ALL RIGHT, HERE WE GO!
Start stretching! It's about to get real.
cue Rocky theme song
ARE YOU READY?!
(please proceed to beat your chest with determination)
THIS IS THE MOMENT!
(would be great if you could clench your fists in preparation)
THE TIME IS NOW!
(initiate heavy breathing—bonus points if you squint)
3... (maybe jump a little)
2... (roaring noises are encouraged)
1...
HERE WE GO!!!! IT'S TIME LIVE A GREAT LIFE.

PART ONE:

In the Beginning

Chapter 1 - Simple! What is that?

The world tries as much as possible to live on simplicity because it paves way for the new to emerge effortlessly.
- Emmer -

Ok, I am naked taking a hot afternoon bathe in a barrel which mum filled with water to the brim. Aha, I realize how simple it is to bathe in this barrel of water which seems like a swimming pool. Why do people even waste their time bathing and soaking up large amount of water with soap when they could do it simply in this barrel of water? I pondered.

I was about the age of six or seven years when that happened. My sister came by and saw spilled water on the floor as a result of the excess volume I created when I dipped myself into the barrel. The floor had wept. I took to my heels while still naked, immediately to avoid being catch. I had DE-sanitized the water with my filth. Buh hey it was simple! I thought.

The notion of simplicity can be an erroneous notion sometimes by humans since we are always finding ways to avoid the hard things in life to settle for the easy and seemingly simple things which are not.

Simple! What is that –

In the context of this book **Simple** streams *from word choices used to elaborate the easiness and reasonable subtleness underlying human thinking efforts and action which humanity believe has caused progression and will continue to evolve humanity as long as we stay hold on to it.*

Now, let me ask you a profound question, have you ever seen a man or a woman on her deathbed passing out to the next life. Now, if you have no idea or if you have, you realized, there are two things which happens. The beautiful soul moving to the next life experience can either have a sensation of unease and struggle or such ease and smooth passage to his or her pathway in the next life. The profound mysteries behind this are sometimes indescribable with words.

A vivid scenario is created when Oprah interviewed a grieving mother whose adult son had passed on after a long illness. You could have heard a pin drop in Oprah's studio when she so beautifully told the story of their final moment together. The mother had climbed into bed with her son. She could barely hear him, but her head was on his chest. As he took his last breath, he whispered, "Oh Mom, it is all so simple. It's so simple, Mom." He then closed his eyes and died.

I got chills when I heard that. I realized then, just as it resonates with me now: We allow life to get so complicated—when it's really so very simple.

From that day forward I resolved to continually ask myself, *how am I making things more difficult than they need to be?*

Your answer to that same question is the next step in your path. It's that simple.

Imagine what lies just around the bend.

Can you see it? I can.

STICK TO SIMPLE IDEAS

"There is a choice you have to make, in everything you do. So, keep in the mind that in the end, the choice you make, makes you."
—Anonymous

I know how much hard work it takes to pursue a dream of building a business. The long hours, time you take away from the family, ideas you know that are brilliant but don't seem to catch on. I remember reading about that and thinking, It's the idea that matters. It didn't matter where you come from or what your background is. One revolutionary idea, one brilliant invention can unleash other entrepreneurs that you never predicted.

Sundar Pichar, CEO – Google

Idea – The invisible force of a visionary or problem-solving thought by man which upon being stirred up by action brings the unknown to known.

Having an idea could be easy. It's easy to have ideas but others find it very difficult to get one, because they are on the verge of difficult ones. Ha-ha! What I have also realized is that, great but simple ideas come from a peaceful mind filled with eagerness of curiosity and creativity bedded with imagination., sometimes, slightly bending the rules.

No doubt about that. To take an idea or product to the marketplace that improves people's lives, requires a lot of hard work.

Be stubborn on your vision. Because otherwise, it would be too easy to give up. But you need to be flexible on the details. It takes persistence, relentlessness.[1]

– You need a combination of stubborn relentlessness and flexibility and know when to be which. Because as you go, you realize that some of your preconceptions were wrong and you need to be able to change them.

You can have creative ideas which can topple up your life in many criteria when you learn to go to your God space – A place of serendipity and peacefulness filled with aha moments, where you normally get struck with a thought and you feel a strong attachment to the thought.

That's why on many cases when one has an idea, people tell them, that's a crazy idea – hey, that won't work – I can tell you; those crazy ideas are always worth it when you execute them.

There is a beautiful ad that Apple used to promote their products in the 90's. I would love to share it with you. It deserves re-stating.

'Here's to us. The crazy ones, the misfits, the rebels, the round pegs in the square hole, the ones who see things differently. We are not fond of the rules and have no respect for the status quo. You can quote us and disagree with us, glorify or vilify us, scrutinize and criticize us. But the only thing you can't do is to ignore us. Because we change things. We intend to push the human race forward. And while some may see me as the crazy ones, some see genius. Because the people who are crazy enough to think that they can change the world are the ones who do.''

I caught you! You felt it, right? It really resonated with you. Yes!

During the play of the ad video, Prominent thinkers including, Albert Einstein, Picasso, Hellen Keller, Richard Branson, Thomas Edison were being used as labels since their ideas, writings or discoveries were first thought as obscure but later turned out to revolutionize the world

Remember – Execution is everything, it what separates the greats from the average.

Sometimes, I wonder if ideas bounce from one head to another, because it seems sometimes an idea that you had formerly had been executed by someone in the latter time but you thought you were the only one who had or conceived it. Hey, I am happy to admit because I have had such experiences.

Guess, what - you might feel like shitting in your pants because you were not bold enough to implement your simple ideas which could have sprout forth to your riches. Don 't let it be you

The secret is that Ideas come with a sense of urgency because they know their time has come.

Never despise Small beginnings – THE GAME CHANGERS

It continues to marvel me in the business world how small businesses rise to form giant corporations in a relative amount of years through hard work, teamwork, culture, speed of technology, taking bold bets/risks ,persistence, stubborn relentlessness, patience, a long-term vision and overcoming insurmountable failures and difficulties which comes with great lessons but can be worth tens, thousands, millions or even trillions of dollars.

Inspired by that, at the time of writing, I have purposed or intended to create a chain of businesses that will improve, evolve and put humanity forward through the invention of products and services, solving problems and chains of helping people from many angles, like my books, time, energy, money but more importantly with compassion, kindness, love , empathy, giving or sharing, etc.

After all, the purpose of existence is primarily, to be ourselves.

This analogy of simple ideas to big realities has been demonstrated in real life by series of companies such as Google, Microsoft, Huawei, Foxconn, ARM, CNN, Amazon, Rakuten, Facebook, Nike, Tesla, Walmart, Adidas, Samsung, Apple, Coca-Cola, Under-Armour, Virgin, Boeing, LVMH, Zara etc. In Scott Galloway book, *The Hidden DNA of the four world-wide companies* he analyses the various companies starting from small beginnings with a vision and mission to pioneer the world in a specific niche.

- **Google** – Organizing the world's information
- **Facebook** – Connecting the world
- **Amazon** – Pioneering online retail
- **Apple** – Offering highest quality products for educational and higher institutions.

As I write this, Jeff Bezos is the wealthiest person in the world. It all started with books. The current gold and silver medallists, Bill Gates and Warren Buffet, are in great businesses (software and insurance), but neither sits on top of a company growing 20 percent plus each year, attacking multibillion-dollar sectors like befuddled prey Amazon- The Earth largest River, hey, now the Earths catalogue of almost every item- *The Everything Store-* As labelled by author *Brad Stone.*

A BRIEF OF THE FOUR

Remember, the beautiful thing about these global companies is that they all started with a simple idea, one computer and a dream with urgency.

Amazon: Founded by *Jeff Bezos* in 1994

Before it was the self-proclaimed largest bookstore on Earth or the Web's dominant superstore, Amazon.com was an idea floating through the New York City offices of one of the most unusual firms on Wall Street: D. E. Shaw & Co.

In 1994, A Texas-based author and publisher named John Quarterman had recently started the *Matrix News,* a monthly newsletter extolling the Internet and discussing its commercial possibilities. One set of numbers in particular in the February 1994 edition of the newsletter was startling.

For the first time, Quarterman broke down the growth of the year-old World Wide Web and pointed out that its simple, friendly interface appealed to a far broader audience than other Internet technologies. In one chart, he showed that the number of bytes—a set of binary digits—transmitted over the Web had increased by a factor of 2,057 between January 1993 and January 1994.

Another graphic showed the number of packets—a single unit of data—sent over the Web had jumped by 2,560 in the same span.

Bezos interpolated from this that Web activity overall had gone up that year by a factor of roughly 2,300—a 230,000 percent increase. "Things just don't grow that fast," Bezos later said. "It's highly unusual, and that started me thinking, what kind of business plan might make sense in the context of that growth?"

(Bezos also liked to say in speeches during Amazon's early years that it was the Web's "2,300 percent" annual growth rate that jolted him out of complacency. Which makes for an interesting historical footnote: Amazon began with a math error.) Bezos concluded that a true everything store would be impractical—at least at the beginning. He made a list of twenty possible product categories, including computer software, office supplies, apparel, and music.

The category that eventually jumped out at him as the best option was **books**.

They were pure commodities; a copy of a book in one store was identical to the same book carried in another, so buyers always knew what they were getting.

There were two primary distributors of books at that time, Ingram and Baker and Taylor, so a new retailer wouldn't have to approach each of the thousands of book publishers individually. And, most important, there were three million books in print worldwide, far more than a Barnes & Noble or a Borders superstore could ever stock.

If he couldn't build a true everything stores right away, he could capture its essence—unlimited selection—in at least one important product category. "With that huge diversity of products, you could build a store online that simply could not exist in any other way," Bezos said. *"You could build a true superstore with exhaustive selection, and customers value selection."*
In his offices on the fortieth floor of 120 West Forty-Fifth Street, Bezos could hardly contain his enthusiasm.

With DESCO's recruiting chief, Charles Ardai, he investigated some of the earliest online bookstore websites, such as Book Stacks Unlimited, located in Cleveland, Ohio, and WordsWorth, in Cambridge, Massachusetts. Ardai still has the record from one purchase they made while testing these early sites.

He bought a copy of *Isaac Asimov's Cyberdreams* from the website of the Future Fantasy bookstore in Palo Alto, California. The price was $6.04. When the book appeared, two weeks later, Ardai ripped open the cardboard package and showed it to Bezos. It had become badly tattered in transit. *No one had yet figured out how to do a good job selling books over the Internet. As Bezos saw it, this was a huge, untapped opportunity.*

Bezos knew it would never really be his company if he pursued the venture inside D. E. Shaw. Indeed, the firm initially owned all of Juno and FarSight, and Shaw acted as chairman of both.

If Bezos wanted to be a true owner and entrepreneur, with significant equity in his creation and the potential to achieve the same kind of financial rewards that businessmen like pizza magnate Frank Meeks did, he had to leave his lucrative and comfortable home on Wall Street.

What happened next became one of the founding legends of the Internet. That spring, Bezos spoke to David Shaw and told him he planned to leave the company to create an online bookstore. Shaw suggested they take a walk. They wandered in Central Park for two hours, discussing the venture and the entrepreneurial drive.

Shaw said he understood Bezos's impulse and sympathized with it—he had done the same thing when he'd left Morgan Stanley. He also noted that D. E. Shaw was growing quickly and that Bezos already had a great job. He told Bezos that the firm might end up competing with his new venture. The two agreed that Bezos would spend a few days thinking about it

At the time Bezos was thinking about what to do next, he had recently finished the novel Remains of the Day, by Kazuo Ishiguro, about a butler who wistfully recalls his personal and professional choices during a career in service in wartime Great Britain. So, looking back on life's important junctures was on Bezos's mind when he came up with what he calls "the regret-minimization framework" to decide the next step to take at this juncture in his career.

"When you are in the thick of things, you can get confused by small stuff," Bezos said a few years later. "I knew when I was eighty that I would never, for example, think about why I walked away from my 1994 Wall Street bonus right in the middle of the year at the worst possible time. That kind of thing just isn't something you worry about when you're eighty years old. At the same time, I knew that I might sincerely regret not having participated in this thing called the Internet that I thought was going to be a revolutionizing event. When I thought about it that way... it was incredibly easy to make the decision." [2]

Now, here is **Amazon** from a simple idea, a non-regrettable decision made by its founder.

Ha-ha! Are you ready for shopping? Shopping for a Porsche Panamera Turbo S or a pair of Louboutin lace pumps is fun. Shopping for toothpaste and eco-friendly diapers is not. As the online retailer of choice for most Americans, and increasingly, the world, Amazon eases the pain of drudgery—getting the stuff you need to survive. No great effort: no hunting, little gathering, just (one) clicking.

Their formula: an unparalleled investment in last-mile infrastructure, made possible by an irrationally generous lender— retail investors who see the most compelling, yet simple, story ever told in business: Earth's Biggest Store.

The story is coupled with execution that rivals D-Day (minus the whole courage and sacrifice to save the world part). The result is a retailer worth more than Walmart, Target, Macy's, Kroger,

Nordstrom, Tiffany & Co., Coach, Williams-Sonoma, Tesco, Ikea, Carrefour, and The Gap combined.

One fascinating thing, I admired about Jeff was when he was being interviewed by David Rubenstein and asked, what do you want your legacy to be on this Earth?

He replied "I want to be the Oldest man who has ever lived". Now, you might be thinking what about his title. None of it serves any relevance to him. He might prefer it if you call him Father, it's okay. He relates relevance to Life- A life fully lived. Now, that is a REAL leader. So, should you be and even better.

Apple:

Founded early on by *Steve Wozniak and late Steve Jobs in 1986*

Today, they're one of the most valuable companies on earth, but how did it all begin? You know what they say—great things happen when you're in the right place at the right time.

The year was 1977, and the timing was perfect for an explosion of innovative technology. A remnant of the '60s counterculture remained in a revolution separate from mainstream America. In tandem with this was the development of the CPU from Intel.

During this time, a sixteen-year-old Steve Jobs met a twenty-one-year-old Steve Wozniak. They were run-of-the-mill university students with a love of technology, pranks, and the Beatles.[3]

Neither of the friends had any idea that the two of them would soon change history.

The Apple logo, which graces the most coveted laptops and mobile devices, is the global badge of wealth, education, and Western values. At its core, Apple fills two instinctual needs: to feel closer to God and be more attractive to the opposite sex. It mimics religion with its own belief system, objects of veneration, cult following, and Christ figure.

It counts among its congregation the most important people in the world: The Innovation Class.

By achieving a paradoxical goal in business—a low-cost product that sells for a premium price—Apple has become the most profitable company in history.

The equivalent is an auto firm with the margins of Ferrari and the production volumes of Toyota. In Q4 of 2016, Apple registered twice the net profits Amazon has produced, in total, since its founding twenty-three years ago. Apple's cash on hand is nearly the GDP of Denmark.

Facebook:

Founded by *Mark Zuckerberg*

As measured by adoption and usage, Facebook is the most successful thing in the history of humankind. There are 7.5 billion people in the world, and 1.2 billion people have a daily relationship with Facebook. Facebook (#1), Facebook Messenger (#2), and Instagram (#8) are the most popular mobile apps in the United States. The social network and its properties register fifty minutes of a user's typical day. One of every six minutes online is spent on Facebook, and one in five minutes spent on mobile is on Facebook.

Google:

Founded by *Sergey Brin and Larry Page*

Google is a modern man's god. It's our source of knowledge—ever-present, aware of our deepest secrets, reassuring us where we are and where we need to go, answering questions from trivial to profound. No institution has the trust and credibility of Google: About one out of six queries posed to the search engine have never been asked before. What rabbi, priest, scholar, or coach has so much gravitas that he or she is presented with that many questions never before asked of anybody? Who else inspires so many queries of the unknown from all corners of the world?

A subsidiary of Alphabet Inc., in 2016 Google earned $20 billion in profits, increased revenues 23 percent, and lowered cost to advertiser's 11 percent—a massive blow to competitors. Google, unlike most products, ages in reverse, becoming more valuable with use. It harnesses the power of 2 billion people, twenty-four hours a day, connected by their intentions (what you want) and decisions (what you chose), yielding a whole infinitely greater than the sum of its parts. The insights into consumer behavior Google gleans from 3.5 billion queries each day make this horseman the executioner of traditional brands and media.

Your new favorite brand is what Google returns to you in .0000005 second.

YOU CAN ALSO OWN A GREAT MASTERPIECE

Now, you might be wondering, these people or companies are being praised like gods. No, they can be god-like, but the reality is they deserved to be given Thankfulness from our hearts.

Or, wait do you want your name to be on World's plaque, boldly written – **Mr. Scott, the world's best entrepreneur ever in modern history** – Well, I have no problem with that, so should you but you should question yourself that " Are you really living a purpose driven life who is not too much excited by awards, accolades and plaques on the wall and almost lives his or her life on those materialistic attitude. If you are doing the opposite, then you know what you are really being and doing.

An amazing personality I love is **John Wooden,**

Early in his career, John Wooden embraced the belief that success, as measured by each one of us individually, is the peace of mind derived from making the absolute and complete *effort* to do the best of which you are capable. The quality of your effort to realize your potential counts first and foremost.

For John Wooden *that* is success. And it is different from winning—beating an opponent in basketball, business, or life.

This is important to recognize: that *success* and *winning* are two very different concepts in the world of Wooden and that success is the foremost of the two. Eddie Powell, a former assistant coach and player, observed, "Coach Wooden was more upset if we won but *didn't* work up to our potential than if we lost playing at our best."

That represents a radically different approach to leadership — a universe apart from "winning is the only thing" or "winning at any cost" or "Just win, baby!"

And yet John Wooden wanted very much to win "every *single* game."

This, of course, is an apparent contradiction in belief and behavior; specifically, Coach Wooden's fierce competitive instinct and desire to win coupled with his deep and abiding conviction that success, as he defines it, supersedes (and often precedes) victory.

Reconciling the two is challenging—to seek winning with all you've got and yet not allow it to be the arbiter of whether you succeed. Nevertheless, to fully appreciate John Wooden's approach to competition, team building, and leadership, you must grasp the fact that he was able to simultaneously and ferociously "play to win" and yet *not* allow the results—the score, trophies, titles, or championships—to be the ultimate measure of his own or his team's success.

He said, " *What is success? For many it's trophies or blue ribbons. That's why this publicity shot was taken—to show how successful our teams had been. But I don't measure it like that. The highest success is in your effort—giving it your personal best.*[4]

I tell you simplifying your life with values, principles, work ethics, well-graded beliefs and a distinct yet impressive attitude not only draws the best to you but more of freshness, understanding and wisdom which many finds it difficult to fathom or comprehend.

Why? Because you Live a simple yet Great Life.

One Thing You Can Do to fulfil this Chapter.

Make your journey of life resonates with who you really are. That's it. Nothing else. Find an idea that you believe in and rock the world with it.

Chapter 2 - What Happened?

When you let go of trying to get more of what you don't really need, it frees up oceans of energy that was caught up in that chase to now turn and pay attention to what you already have. When you actually pay attention to, nourish, love, and share what you already have, it expands. It's the opposite of what we think. And when people know that, it frees them from this chase of more, more, more, more, more. A shorter way to say all that is, what you appreciate, appreciates.

- Lynn Twist -

Never judge a man based on his appearance. Well, that's so easy to say. Consequently, what will be the right way? The right way is don't judge at all but your answer or responsiveness must solely come from intuitive conclusion. You will almost know a person very well by great observation and a little intuition.

Many great men and women have lost it all, because they never sensed enough. Come to think of this in this way, Life is like the World Wide Web. There is a great massive connection bundled with great amount of data. Now, you might be thinking how the hell is the earth connected instantly with the advent of the Internet. Yes, it is. A complicated life can look like the internet on the backend where you don't see what goes on entirely.

It all comes to the BETTER situation where these men and women evolve their experience by sharing. By contributing. By serving. By nourishing other people. That's where real prosperity lives.

Have you ever been in a conversation where you realized an admirable personality of yours lost a great deal of his wealth and unfortunately crumbled into the streets as a beggar and if not lost his or true sense of purpose?

SPIRAL MOMENTS IN LIFE

Let me tell you something, one of the most memorable examples of the dangers of allowing material achievement to dictate self-worth is the story of author *Sarah Ban Breathnach*. I've said for years that Sarah's best-selling book *Simple Abundance* is the reason I started keeping a gratitude journal; it changed the way I moved through the world. *Simple Abundance* sold seven million copies, and before she knew it, Sarah was a multimillionaire. As a bonafide publishing superstar, she hired nine assistants, brought home eight pairs of Manolo Blahnik shoes in one trip, and bought the actual chapel once owned by Sir Isaac Newton. But fifteen years later Sarah joined Oprah for a moving conversation in which she courageously shared the story of how she lost it all—and what she eventually gained in return.

What I learned from Sarah and so many others is that the way people handle money reflects the way they see themselves. Many times, when people win the lottery and experience a windfall, they don't see themselves as worthy of their newfound riches.

They wind up spending on possessions to create an idea of self-worth. When you've become blinded by the status symbols, it's easy to lose sight of the unique gifts only you can offer the world.

What I know for sure is that no matter how much wealth you come to possess, everything passes and changes with time.

What is real, what is forever, is who you are and what you are meant to share with the world.

That is your true treasure.

MYSTERIES OF THE WORLD

Unlocking the mysteries behind the world would take thousands of years to come. Man has unravelled many discoveries but I can confidently tell you that many unforeseen events which have not yet happen and will happen will spike the distance between the human mind and the faculty of human imagined limited possibilities.

The billions of people who have died and gone paved this moment that you and I are experiencing. Have you mused on the very thought of what the old people of our past generations would have said if they were in your time at this particular moment in time and space? I can vividly tell you; this would be their response. What an amazing world you have. How on earth did you get here! A probable response would be Its "Natures simplified way of evolving".

As the legendary poet Woodsworth, tells first how in his youth, Nature was all in all to him, "nor needed a moral sense unborrowed from the eye," but later the inner light came; and hear him in his mature years: saying:

> "For I have learned
> To look on Nature, not as in the hour
> Of thoughtless youth; but hearing oftentimes
> The still, sad music of humanity,
> Nor harsh nor grating, though of ample power
> To chasten and subdue. And I have felt
> A Presence that disturbs me with the joy
> Of elevated thoughts; a sense sublime
> Of something far more deeply interfused,
> Whose dwelling is the light of setting suns,
> And the round ocean and the living air,
> And the blue sky, and in the mind of man;
> A motion and a spirit, that impels
> All thinking things, all objects of all thought,
> And rolls through all things."

If we go higher still in the scale, we find that the companionship of the gods is not denied to the steady wage-receiving man, for Shakespeare, Burns and Scott can be had for six pence per volume. In this blessed age in which we are privileged to live, even the immortals are cheap and visit the toiler.

We see the rich rolling over the land in their limousines, but blessed beyond these is the man who strolls along the hedge-rows. The connoisseur in his gallery misses the health-giving breeze which brings happiness to the devotee who seeks the original afield.

The lady in her overheated conservatory knows nothing of the joyous rapture of her more fortunate sister who gathers the spoils of the glen.

Ah, my friends, ponder well over this truth: the more one dwells with her, the more one draws from her, the closer one creeps to her bosom, the sweeter is nature's kiss.

From man's neglect of her for meaner substitutes come most of the disappointment and unhappiness of life.

The masses of mankind are happy all round the world because their pleasures are drawn so largely from sources which lie open to all. The rich are not to be envied, for truly "there is no purchase in money" of any real happiness.

When used for our own gratification, it injures us; when used ostentatiously, it brings care; when hoarded, it narrows the soul. Nature has not provided a means by which any man can use riches for selfish purposes without suffering therefrom.

There is only one source of true blessedness in wealth, and that comes from giving it away for ends that tend to elevate our brothers and enable them to share it with us. Nature is gloriously communistic after all, God bless her! and sees that a pretty fair division is made, let man hoard as he may. The secret of happiness is renunciation and simplicity.

The unprecedented advance made by western nations in the past and present generations, upon which we continually plume ourselves, is shared by the world in general. Wherever we have been, one story met us. Everywhere there is progress, not only material but intellectual as well, and rapid progress too.

The oldest inhabitant has always his comparison to offer between the days of his youth and the advantages possessed by the youth of to-day. Matters are not as they were. We saw no race which had retrograded, if we except Ghana, which is now in a transitional state, and will ultimately prove no exception to the rule.

The whole world moves, and moves in the right direction—upward and onward—the things that are better than those that have been and those to come to be better than those of to-day.

The law of evolution—the higher from the lower—is not discredited by a voyage round the world and the knowledge of what is transpiring around us.

I have made it my goal to travel around the world to as many countries as I can, assiduously to create businesses but moreover to connect with a long fellow brother or sister in a foreign country who has been waiting for me from the beginning of time. I have come to realize based on other people's experiences that glorious nature one way or the other has hidden simple pearls of wisdom and ideas like goldmine around the world.

In Andrew Carnegie's book, *Round the World*, he elaborates on his journey around the world as he experiences shock and awe through the strength, thankfulness and kindness people had despite their perils.

''The trip has been without a single unpleasant incident. We have not missed one connection, nor ever been beyond the reach of all the comforts of life, nor have we had one unhappy or even lonely hour. Every day has brought

something new or interesting. And sitting here in our quiet mountain home this morning, I feel that there is scarcely a prize that could be offered for which I would exchange the knowledge obtained and the memories of things seen during my trip. One of the great pleasures of travel in the East is the unbounded hospitality—excessive kindness—everywhere met with. Will the numerous kind friends to whom we are so deeply indebted—a host far too great to name—please accept this general acknowledgment as at least a slight evidence that their goodness to us is not unappreciated? At every stage of our travels I have been struck with the cheering thought, that notwithstanding the indisputable fact that a vast amount of misery seems inseparable from human life, still the general condition of mankind is a happy one. No matter who or what he is, the man of the East in his heart exalts his own country and his own race, and esteems them specially favored of the gods. And indeed, it is with nations as with individuals: as none are entirely good, so none are entirely bad. The unseen power is at work in all lands, evolving the higher from the lower and steadily improving all, so the traveller finds much to commend in every country, and seeing this he grows tolerant and liberal, and able more heartily to sing.''[5]

BEING AN UNDERDOG

When I look back into the past, in my years at High School, it was like the tides of the ocean. I was a good student. I really learnt hard but not in a smart way (that was my bad) to the extent that sometimes I missed bathing periods. Ugh, I don't think that was good, right?

Well, in my school, there were many classmates of mine that did that awful thing, but I realized it seems normal to them. It, took a long time for me to change.

They had a term called "Brilla" to denote someone was an excellent student. There were students of mine who were publicly known to be academically good but there were others who were almost not known, but guess what? They were real sharks. These people, I called them, the underdogs.

In every setting that they presented themselves, they were very simple, humble in their dealings and seems to always know when to do something and when not to initiate. Being an underdog, I can tell you is really fun. Was I an underdog then, No. But I learnt how to be one in the light not in the shadows.

My friends usually hooted at me because they were very pessimistic about my way of studying and some often thought I was flaunting too much. Those days gave me hardcore lessons on the effective and resilient way of conducting myself in diligence.

Today, I can confidently tell you what life can be like if you decide to live your life where you are able to correct people in private and praise them in public, not only would you be highly respected but you would have a resonance.

Being an underdog, can serve a huge purpose, because whatever is being done is not for fame or strictly publicity but for the reality that it must be done, period – no matter what people talk behind your backs.

The is a brief conversational between Oprah and Alanis Morrissette as she elaborates on what really matters in life. It's worth taking.

ALANIS MORISSETTE: *I thought that all would be helped and healed and soothed by fame.*

OPRAH: *Because you believed, When I get famous ...*

ALANIS: *I will be less lonely. And I will be understood and I will be loved and that love will go in and heal any of the broken parts.*

OPRAH: *And the truth is, there's no difference between fame or, thoughts like, When I get thin, or, When I get rich, or, When I meet the right guy.*

ALANIS: *When I get that job. Yes. When I have babies. When I retire.*

OPRAH: *Then I will be happy. I will be healed. It's all the same thing.*

ALANIS: *And everything will be okay. Yes. As though somehow, we as humans could be exempt from pain. You know, one of the big lessons I've learned has been that if I can be comfortable with pain, which is different from suffering, but comfortable with pain as just an indication. And, it's potentially a daily thing, in my case, then there won't be my living in the future all the time. That one day if and when I'll be happy and that on the other side there is this great sense of peace.*

One Thing You Can Do to fulfil this Chapter of your life.

―――――――――――――――

*Analyse and place yourself in a momentary pause. Think, and ask yourself – What clutter and notion of beliefs am I restricting myself with? then **DEAL** with it accordingly.*

―――――――――

Chapter 3- Sitting on the Bench.

Here's the question. *What have I come here to do with my life?* That's the question that begins every single quest. *What have I come here to do with my life?* There's no one who hasn't had that question come to them. That's the call. Now, you can choose to ignore that question or you can pursue it. And the pursuit is the beginning of the journey.
- *Elizabeth Gilbert* –

The simple act of asking "What is my purpose?" on the Internet has the power to elicit nearly one *billion* responses.

That's a staggering commentary on the way so many people feel about who they are and how much they long for an existence that matters.

On the surface, typing those four little words ... *what—is—my—purpose* ... and pressing Enter may seem trivial, but it's really a profound reflection of an intimate prayer rising from the deepest part of the heart. It's asking to be acknowledged. Initiating that search is a sign that the journey toward an elevated life filled with meaning and character is ready to begin.

And here is the *great* news. Beyond the labyrinth of digital links, there is really just one being who holds the keys to unlock the answers to all that you were meant to become. That miraculous soul has been speaking your entire life. Of course, I'm talking about you!

I believe every one of us is born with a purpose. No matter who you are, what you do, or how far you think you have to go, you have been tapped by a force greater than yourself to step into your God-given calling.

This goes far beyond what you do to earn your living. I'm talking about a supreme moment of destiny, the reason you are here on earth.

Each one of us has an essential role in the whole of humanity. All you have to do is follow your path to answer the call.

In the words of the Chinese philosopher Lao-tzu, *A journey of a thousand miles begins with a single step.*

My hope with **Simple, yet Great** is to offer the wisdom of experience from myself, the visionaries, artists, teachers, and trailblazers who have walked this road before you, and who have shared their inspiration and lessons with us prompting us every awaking moment to remember to live a life worth lived. The common thread among them: They have discovered that in this world, there is no real *doing* without first *being.*

Within these pages, you will find a guide to activating every layer of the miracle that makes you uniquely you—and applying it to the life you envision.

Committing to a life of purpose takes courage. There was a time in my own life when I felt torn between who the world was telling me I should be and what I felt to be the truth of myself.

Today, I know for sure what I'm here to do. That's because I started listening to my instincts and paying attention to the decisions, I made each and every day. I am the sum of my choices.

If you're at a crossroads in your career or relationship, if you're struggling with finances, with addiction, or to take control of your health, the journey to lasting change begins with defining what matters most to you.

All of us have a limited number of years here on earth. What do you want to do with yours? How do you want to spend your precious, ever-unfolding future? There's no need to waste another day wondering if there's more to life. There is. And it's yours for the finding. When you're ready.

An UNTOLD STORY

My story began in the suburbs of Afrancho, a locality within the city of Kumasi in Ghana. There is an adage that says that everybody has a story to tell, but my story might be a little piercing as compared to your story.

A dark cloud had invaded my family causing a sad occurring divorce between my parents. My father had remarried after some years and my mother was to cater for seven kids. I always knew the pain she was passing through but will always keep the dilemma to herself.

She didn't want any of us to worry about it in anyway. She was in a bread business. She had to exports loads of breads in wooden boxes to make a living for us. Gods' hand kept her going all the time.

EDUCATION LADDER CRUMBLING

My stay in High School was unfortunate sometimes, since I had to deal with obstructed flow of payment of fees. The crispy and profound moments always continue to unfold as mum strived to thrive as she can to pass me through three solid years – still she was left to provide for the family entirely.

I had completed Senior High School and had passed excellently with highly commendable results. I was stuck, I couldn't further my education.

The very educational opportunities were a hotshot for most of my colleagues as they entered successfully but some also struggled well than me. Well, I couldn't get funded entirely by my parents then and had to go in for a job.

There were times in my family where we were on tough backslides, events where I remember she would complain of her money being robbed by which was duly allocated for her suppliers in business. She was harnessed emotionally and had to rise.

In spite of all these; she went on finding and discovering portals of keeping the family on track. She was very persistent and forceful. I was able to make it to the University because I believed.

Abraham Lincoln said " All that I am, I owe it to my mother – I seem to understand why Mother's Day are highly celebrated than Fathers. If you are a mother or a lady reading this, I sincerely say God bless you for your futuristic love for your kids or family.

A SUICIDAL THOUGHT –

Years after graduating from school, I was in a midst of depression and burdened on the hearts with suicidal thoughts because I just couldn't find any reason to live.

I was bombarded with thoughts of evil conviction of unworthiness. Unfortunately, I kept finding reasons to believe that.

One darkish night, when all had settled, I found myself hanging on a rope tied to my neck. There was an immense flow of inappropriate and whispering voices that took me out of the real phase of my heart and landing me in my deepest negative self. I was lost.

Through God's intervention, the rope slung anonymously from my neck without any act on my part. I fell down. I cried all I can. I t was one of the painful yet memorable events in my life.

People around the house who heard the news, came and consoled me and reminded me of **WHAT I WAS FOR, MY LIFE, DESTINY** or **PURPOSE** and the trajectory of the shot of adventure that life has paved for me only if I was ready to become myself and be who I was originally intended to be.

Writing this book reminds me that I still have a simple life to live and should not make it complicated in any way. So, should you.

When I read a script, either my skin tingles, or my stomach churns. It's that simple. If my skin tingles, I know it's something I must do. If my stomach churns, I know it is something I cannot do. I have learned something from every single character that I've played. Something emotionally, spiritually, and psychologically true. I've never done a job just for money. I could not do anything that would not enhance humanity, especially for women.
It's so easy when the money is flashed before you to allow that to govern your choices. But it's more important to me to have peace of mind, body, and soul than to have all of the riches. When I put my head on my pillow at night, I don't require a drug, alcohol, or anything else. Just fatigue. - **Cicely Tyson**

IS IT ENOUGH?

Wow, money is cool – Right, when people ask me – When are you going to have more money? I reply " I already have more, more money is amazing – It gives freedom, power, fame, sexiness and more choices but it doesn't entirely give you peace of mind when you are so much attached to it.

A granular amount of money you have must be appreciated, when you don't have at all – Thank the universe for providing you with abundance even though you don't see it but you believe it and keep working because it's a gift. A simple life knows that everything is already here and has been there before the beginning of time.
I like to think of it this way – I am all that is. ALL! Yes, everything – There are huge goals in my life that I intend to achieve, honestly, they are necessary because it helps awakens and evolves me in many facets of experiencing life fully before

death. Unfortunately, few experience a fully lived life because you will always know it when is either way.

A dialogue between Oprah and Lynne Twist sums it all.

LYNNE TWIST: I've learned a great deal from the people I used to call poor and the people I used to call rich. And now I just realize we're all whole and complete people living in the ebb and flow of financial circumstances that change all the time and do not define us.

OPRAH: I thought it was interesting how you say we question everything else. We question race, religion, other life circumstances. But money—we just give it the power.

LYNNE: It's not that we have it. It has us. And we've assigned it more power than human life. More power than the natural world. More power than our relationships with each other. And we all know that's not true. But we live as if money's more important than anything else. And it cripples us. It gives us tremendous anxiety and suffering. Somehow, we drop this wonderful sense of value and worth and love and relationship that we have in the rest of life and we become irritable and competitive and greedy. There is so much suffering in this world in people's relationship with money. There's lying. There are things people wish they had never done. Things they didn't do that they wish they had done. You know, everybody has baggage.

OPRAH: Because of the silent power of money. That's what you call it.

LYNNE: Yes, we just think it will resolve everything. Everybody thinks, Well, if I just had 30 percent more, everything would be fine. But 30 percent ago, it wasn't fine. So, 30 percent more won't really do it. Because when you get there, you want 30 percent more. We're just completely addicted in a society that values money above all else. And it's hurtful. It wounds us.

OPRAH: So, in order to break that scarcity myth, that belief that there's not enough, you say we need to live in the place of sufficiency.

LYNNE: Yes. Sufficiency is a place of wholeness and completeness and deep understanding of who we are. And it's almost impossible to get to enough-ness or sufficiency in a world that exalts what I call the "myth of scarcity"—which is a mind-set, an unconscious, unexamined set of assumptions of "not enough." There's not enough time. There's not enough money. There's not enough love. There are not enough vacations. There's not enough sex. There's not enough this. There's not enough that. And every meeting, every conversation, every lunch, every dinner, every everything is about what we don't have enough of. It's the siren song of a consumer culture. It's not just about money. It dribbles over into every aspect of life.

OPRAH: Everything.

LYNNE: *Yes. It's not just there is not enough, it's not enough. We're not enough. I'm not enough. And that deficit relationship with ourselves is the source of so much of our suffering. It comes from this unconscious, unexamined mind-set I call "scarcity," which has made up these myths. There is not enough to go around. And someone somewhere is always going to be left out.*

OPRAH: And if you believe that, and buy into that, then that's exactly what you will create.

LYNNE: Exactly. It gives people permission to accumulate way more than they need out of the fear that they're not going to have enough. So even massive accumulation often comes from the fear I'm not going to have enough for me.

LIFE IS NOT MEANT TO BE DIFFICULT.

Life is really an amazing journey that we all have to share. Anita Morjani, a survivor of a near death experience after going through a serious stage four cancer comes back to elaborate the necessity of streamlining our life down to a path of simplicity where greatness is assured since the imprint of life was not meant to be a struggle but unfortunately we have created our experiences(that we are having in the now. Anita Morjani was born in Singapore of Indian parents, moved to Hong Kong at the age of two, and has lived in Hong Kong most of her life. Because of her background and British education, she is multilingual and grew up speaking English, Cantonese, and an Indian dialect simultaneously; she later learned French at school. Anita had been working in the corporate world for many years before being diagnosed with cancer in April 2002. Her fascinating and moving near-death experience in early 2006 tremendously changed her perspective on life, and her work is now ingrained with the depths and insights she gained while in the other realm.

When she was being asked that "Is it her opinion that before we take physical form, we're already magnificent beings completely aware of who we truly are? If so, how does our magnificence get eroded and our sense of self become so damaged when we come into this life?

She responded, saying;

"I'll tell you what I feel, but I think it will only raise more questions than answers! It seemed to me that we aren't meant to forget who we are, and that life isn't meant to be so difficult. It felt as though we made it tough here with our misplaced ideas and beliefs.

The internal understanding I received in that realm came as sort of an "imprint," but if I put a voice to it, here's what I would have been saying internally in that state: Ooh, so life isn't supposed to be such a struggle— we're supposed to enjoy it and have fun! I wish I'd known this! Oh, so my body created the cancer because of all my dumb thoughts, judgments about myself, limiting beliefs, all of which caused me so much internal turmoil. Boy, if only I'd known that we're just supposed to come here and feel good about ourselves and about life—just express ourselves and have fun with it!

Now this part is a little hard to explain, but let me try. I had a question that was something like this: Why did something so big—like this terminal cancer thing—happen to me just for not realizing my own magnificence?

Simultaneously, I had this understanding: Ooh, I see—it didn't happen to me, because in truth, I'm never a victim. The cancer is just my own unexpressed power and energy! It turned inward against my body, rather than outward.

I knew it wasn't a punishment or anything like that. It was just my own life force expressing itself as cancer because I didn't allow it to manifest as the magnificent, powerful force of Anita. I was aware that I had a choice as to whether I wanted to come back into my body or go onward into death. The cancer would no longer be there because the energy was no longer expressing itself that way but was going to be present as my infinite self.

I came back with the understanding that heaven truly is a state and not a place, and I've found that bliss has followed me here to Earth. I know this sounds really strange, but I even feel that our "true home" is also only a way of being and not a location. Right now, I feel that I'm home. I have no desire to be anywhere else. It makes no difference to me now whether I'm here or in the other realm. It's all just different parts of the experience of our greater, expanded, infinite, magnificent self. Our real home is within each of us and follows us wherever we go.''

Today, Anita is preaching to the masses in her videos and speaking conferences why we should be really true to ourselves. I always hear the notion of be yourself but it seems people don't really get the context of it.

I would therefore render a very strong idea behind being yourself and being true to yourself. Now, what matters is how you feel about yourself, right here and right now, because that's what determines how you conduct your life here. There's no time except the present moment, so it's important to be yourself and live your own truth. Passionate scientists living from their magnificence are as valuable to humankind as a whole room full of Mother Teresas.

Always remember not to give away your power—instead, get in touch with your own magnificence. When it comes to finding the right path, there's a different answer for each person. The only universal solution I have is to love yourself unconditionally and be yourself fearlessly!

When we're true to ourselves, we become instruments of truth for the planet. Because we're all connected, we touch the lives of everyone around us, who then affect others. Our only obligation is to be the love we are and allow our answers to come from within in the way that's most appropriate for us.

Finally, I can't stress enough how important it is to enjoy yourself and not take yourself or life too seriously. One of the biggest flaws with many traditional spiritual systems is that they often make us take life too seriously. Although I abhor creating doctrines, if I ever had to create a set of tenets for a spiritual path to healing, number one on my list would be to make sure *to laugh as often as possible throughout every single day*— ha-ha! and preferably laugh at myself. This would be hands down over and above any form of prayer, meditation, chanting, or diet reform. Day-to-day problems never seem as big when viewed through a veil of humor and love.

In this age of information technology, we're bombarded with news seemingly at the speed of light. We're living in an age of high stress and fear, and in the midst of trying to protect ourselves from everything we think is "out there," we've forgotten to enjoy ourselves and to take care of what's inside.

Our life is our prayer. It's our gift to this universe, and the memories we leave behind when we someday exit this world will be our legacy to our loved ones. We owe it to ourselves and to everyone around us to be happy and to spread that joy around.

If we can go through life armed with humor and the realization that we are love, we'll already be ahead of the game. Add a box of good chocolates into the mix, and we've really got a winning formula!

I wish you joy as you realize your magnificence and express yourself fearlessly in the world for that will not only earn you a simple life but a life of mastery and excellence.

One Thing You Can Do to fulfil this Chapter of your life.

Laugh every moment you can find and don't take life too seriously. Appreciate every moment you find like a flow of water. Be water.

Chapter 4 – Simple Living

The cause of all problems in this world is ignorance. The solution is Awareness and Remembrance.

- Unknown –

Simple living encompasses a number of different voluntary practices to simplify one's lifestyle. These may include, for example,

- reducing one's possessions
- generally referred to as minimalism
- or increasing self-sufficiency.

Simple living may be characterized by individuals being satisfied with what they have rather than want. Although asceticism generally promotes living simply and refraining from luxury and indulgence, not all proponents of simple living are ascetics. Simple living is distinct from those living in forced poverty, as it is a voluntary lifestyle choice.

Adherents may choose simple living for a variety of personal reasons, such as spirituality, health, increase in quality time for family and friends, work–life balance, personal taste, financial sustainability, frugality, or reducing stress.

Simple living can also be a reaction to materialism and conspicuous consumption. Some cite socio-political goals aligned with the environmentalist, anti-consumerist or anti-war movements, including conservation, degrowth, social justice, and tax resistance.

Religious and spiritual

A number of religious and spiritual traditions encourage simple living. Early examples include *the Śramaṇa traditions of Iron Age India, Gautama Buddha, and biblical Nazirites (notably John the Baptist).* The biblical figure **Jesus** is said to have lived a simple life. He is said to have encouraged his disciples "to take nothing for their journey except a staff—no bread, no bag, no money in their belts — but to wear sandals and not put on two tunics." Various notable individuals have claimed that spiritual inspiration led them to a simple living lifestyle, such as **Benedict of Nursia, Francis of Assisi, Ammon Hennacy, Leo Tolstoy, Rabindranath Tagore, Albert Schweitzer, and Mahatma Gandhi.**

Traditions of simple living stretch back to antiquity, finding resonance with leaders such as **Zarathustra, Buddha, Laozi, and Confucius and Jesus** were heavily stressed in both Greco-Roman culture and Judeo-Christian ethics. Diogenes, a major figure in the ancient Greek philosophy of Cynicism, claimed that a simple life was necessary for virtue, and was said to have lived in a wine jar.

Plain people are Christian groups who have for centuries practiced lifestyles in which some forms of wealth or technology are excluded for religious or philosophical reasons. Groups include the Shakers, Mennonites, Amish, Hutterites, Amana Colonies, Bruderhof, Old German Baptist Brethren, Harmony Society, and some Quakers. There is a Quaker belief called Testimony of simplicity that a person ought to live her or his life simply.

Jean-Jacques Rousseau strongly praised the simple life in many of his writings, especially in his Discourse on the Arts and Sciences (1750) and Discourse on Inequality

Secular

Epicureanism, based on the teachings of the Athens-based philosopher Epicurus, flourished from about the fourth century BC to the third century AD. Epicureanism upheld the untroubled life as the paradigm of happiness, made possible by carefully considered choices. Specifically, Epicurus pointed out that troubles entailed by maintaining an extravagant lifestyle tend to outweigh the pleasure of partaking in it. He therefore concluded that *what is necessary for happiness, bodily comfort, and life itself should be maintained at minimal cost, while all things beyond what is necessary for these should either be tempered by moderation or completely avoided.*

Reconstruction of Henry David Thoreau's cabin on the shores of Walden Pond.

Henry David Thoreau, an American naturalist and author, is often considered to have made the classic secular statement advocating a life of simple and sustainable living in his book *Walden* (1854). Thoreau conducted a two-year experiment living a plain and simple life on the shores of Walden Pond.

In Victorian Britain, Henry Stephens Salt, an admirer of Thoreau, popularised the idea of "Simplification, the saner method of living". Other British advocates of the simple life included Edward Carpenter, William Morris, and the members of the "Fellowship of the New Life". Carpenter popularised the phrase the "Simple Life" in his essay *Simplification of Life* in his England's Ideal (1887).

C.R. Ashbee and his followers also practiced some of these ideas, thus linking simplicity with the Arts and Crafts movement. British novelist John Cowper Powys advocated the simple life in his 1933 book A Philosophy of Solitude. John Middleton Murry and Max Plowman practised a simple lifestyle at their Adelphi Centre in Essex in the 1930s. Irish poet Patrick Kavanagh championed a *"right simplicity"* philosophy based on ruralism in some of his work.

George Lorenzo Noyes, a naturalist, mineralogist, development critic, writer, and artist, is known as the Thoreau of Maine. He lived a wilderness lifestyle, advocating through his creative work a simple life and reverence for nature. During the 1920s and 1930s, the Vanderbilt Agrarians of the Southern United States advocated a lifestyle and culture centered upon traditional and sustainable agrarian values as opposed to the progressive urban industrialism which dominated the Western world at that time.

Thorstein Veblen warned against the conspicuous consumption of the materialistic society with The Theory of the Leisure Class (1899); Richard Gregg coined the term "voluntary simplicity" in

The Value of Voluntary Simplicity (1936). From the 1920s, a number of modern authors articulated both the theory and practice of living simply, among them Gandhian Richard Gregg, economists Ralph Borsodi and Scott Nearing, anthropologist-poet Gary Snyder, and utopian fiction writer Ernest Callenbach. E. F. Schumacher argued against the notion that "bigger is better" in Small Is Beautiful (1973); and Duane Elgin continued the promotion of the simple life in Voluntary Simplicity (1981).

The Australian academic Ted Trainer practices and writes about simplicity, and established The Simplicity Institute at Pigface Point, some 20 km from the University of New South Wales to which it is attached. A secular set of nine values was developed with the *Ethify Yourself project* in Austria, having a simplified life style in mind and accompanied by an online book (2011).

In the United States voluntary simplicity started to garner more public exposure through a movement in the late 1990s around a popular "simplicity" book, **The Simple Living Guide** by Janet Luhrs. Around the same time, minimalism (a similar movement) started to also show its light into the public eye.

Changing mindset

Living simply involves different lifestyle habits. When trying to achieve a simple living lifestyle, the idea of it sounds satisfying, but the essence of this practice is to do it repeatedly.

Danny Dover, Author of book *"The Minimalist Mindset"*, states ideas are simply just thoughts, but implementing and acting on these ideas in our own lives is what will make it habitual, and allowing a change in mindset. Leo Babauta believes finding beauty and joy in less, is what advocates the thought of "more is better" to be untrue.

It is quality over quantity that minimalists prefer to follow. There is meaning and what they own holds a true value to them rather than just having things to have. This mindset has spread among many individuals due to influences of other people living this lifestyle.

Joshua Millburn and Ryan Nicodemus share their story of what they used to see life for. The constant additions that are never ending in these worlds are what drove their impulses to keep buying and filling this void of acceptance and approval. Realizing there was this emptiness of being able to get anything they want, there was no meaning behind what they had. This called for a change in mindset with what they see as important and truly valuable before they can begin any other practices or lifestyle habits.

Reducing consumption, work time, and possessions

"Simplicity boils down to two steps: Identify the essential. Eliminate the rest."

Leo Babauta

Some people practice simple living by reducing consumption. By lowering expenditure on goods or services, the time spent earning money can be reduced. The time saved may be used to pursue other interests, or help others through volunteering.

Some may use the extra free time to improve their quality of life, for example pursuing creative activities such as art and crafts. Developing a detachment from money has led some individuals, such as Suelo and Mark Boyle, to live with no money at all.

Reducing expenses may also lead to increasing savings, which can lead to financial independence and the possibility of early retirement.

"You have succeeded in life when all you really want is only what you really need.

Vernon Howard"

The 100 Thing Challenge is a grassroots movement to whittle down personal possessions to one hundred items, with the aim of decluttering and simplifying life. The small house movement includes individuals who chose to live in small, mortgage-free, low-impact dwellings, such as log cabins or beach huts.

Those who follow simple living may hold a different value over their homes. **Joshua Becker** suggests simplifying the place that they live for those who desire to live this lifestyle. He addresses the fact that the purpose of a home is a place for safety and belonging.

Many get caught up over all of the space they have in their house and feel the need to buy stuff to fill it. This is something that must be reflected upon because it raises the question of if it is just pleasing to the eye, or if it is truly needed.

Increasing self-sufficiency

Robert Hart's forest garden in Shropshire, England, UK

One way to simplify life is to get back-to-the-land and grow your own food, as increased self-sufficiency reduces dependency on money and the economy.

Tom Hodgkinson believes the key to a free and simple life is to stop consuming and start producing. This is a sentiment shared by an increasing number of people, including those belonging to the millennial generation such as writer and eco blogger **Jennifer Nini,** who left the city to live off-grid, grow food, and "be a part of the solution; not part of the problem.

Forest gardening, developed by simple living adherent Robert Hart, is a low-maintenance plant-based food production system based on woodland ecosystems, incorporating fruit and nut trees, shrubs, herbs, vines and perennial vegetables. Hart created a model forest garden from a 0.12-acre orchard on his farm at Wenlock Edge in Shropshire. The idea of food miles, the number of miles a given item of food or its ingredients has travelled between the farm and the table, is used by simple living advocates to argue for locally grown food.

This is now gaining mainstream acceptance, as shown by the popularity of books such as the 100-Mile Diet, and Barbara Kingsolver's Animal, Vegetable, Miracle: A Year of Food Life. In each of these cases, the authors devoted a year to reducing their carbon footprint by eating locally.

City dwellers can also produce fresh home-grown fruit and vegetables in pot gardens or miniature indoor greenhouses. Tomatoes, lettuce, spinach, Swiss chard, peas, strawberries, and several types of herbs can all thrive in pots. Jim Merkel says that a person "could sprout seeds. They are tasty, incredibly nutritious, and easy to grow... We grow them in wide mouthed mason jars with a square of nylon window screen screwed under a metal ring". Farmer Matt Moore spoke on this issue: "How does it affect the consumer to know that broccoli takes 105 days to grow a head? The supermarket mode is one of plenty — it's always stocked. And that changes our sense of time. How long it takes to grow food — that's removed in the marketplace. They don't want you to think about how long it takes to grow, because they want you to buy right now". One way to change this viewpoint is also suggested by Mr. Moore. He placed a video installation in the produce section of a grocery store that documented the length of time it took to grow certain vegetables. This aimed to raise awareness in people of the length of time actually needed for gardens.

The do it yourself ethic refers to the principle of undertaking necessary tasks oneself rather than having others, who are more skilled or experienced, complete them for you.

Reconsidering technology

People who practice simple living have diverse views on the role of technology. The American political activist Scott Nearing was sceptical about how humanity would use new technology, citing destructive inventions such as nuclear weapons. Those who eschew modern technology are often referred to as Luddites or neo-Luddites.

Although simple living is often a secular pursuit, it may still involve reconsidering personal definitions of appropriate technology, as Anabaptist groups such as the Amish or Mennonites have done.

Technological proponents see cutting-edge technologies as a way to make a simple lifestyle within mainstream culture easier and more sustainable. They argue that the internet can reduce an individual's carbon footprint through telecommuting and lower paper usage. Some have also calculated their energy consumption and have shown that one can live simply and in an emotionally satisfying way by using much less energy than is used in Western countries. Technologies they may embrace include computers, photovoltaic systems, wind and water turbines.

Technological interventions that appear to simplify living may actually induce side effects elsewhere or at a future point in time. Evgeny Morozov warns that tools like the internet can facilitate mass surveillance and political repression. The book **Green Illusions** identifies how wind and solar energy technologies have hidden side effects and can actually increase energy consumption and entrench environmental harms over time. Authors of the book Techno-Fix criticize technological optimists for overlooking the limitations of technology in solving agricultural problems.

Advertising is criticised for encouraging a consumerist mentality. Many advocates of simple living tend to agree that cutting out, or cutting down on, television viewing is a key ingredient in simple living. Some see the Internet, podcasting, community radio, or pirate radio as viable alternatives.

Simplifying diet

Another practice is the adoption of a simplified diet. Diets that may simplify domestic food production and consumption include vegan diets and the Gandhi diet. In the United Kingdom, the Movement for Compassionate Living was formed by Kathleen and Jack Jannaway in 1984 to spread the vegan message and promote simple living and self-reliance as a remedy against the exploitation of humans, animals, and the Earth

Environmentalism

Simple living may be undertaken by environmentalists. For example, Green parties often advocate simple living as a consequence of their *"four pillars"* or the *"Ten Key Values"* of the Green Party of the United States. This includes, in policy terms, their rejection of genetic engineering and nuclear power and other technologies they consider to be hazardous.

The Greens' support for simplicity is based on the reduction in natural resource usage and environmental impact. This concept is expressed in Ernest Callenbach's "green triangle" of ecology, frugality and health.

The White House Peace Vigil, started by simple living adherent Thomas in 1981.

Many with similar views avoid involvement even with green politics as compromising simplicity, however, and advocate forms of green anarchism that attempt to implement these principles at a smaller scale, e.g. the ecovillage. Deep ecology, a belief that the world does not exist as a resource to be freely exploited by humans, proposes wilderness preservation, human population control and simple living.

Anti-war

The alleged relationship between economic growth and war, when fought for control and exploitation of natural and human resources, is considered a good reason for promoting a simple living lifestyle.

Avoiding the perpetuation of the resource curse is a similar objective of many simple living adherents.

Opposition to war has led peace activists, such as **Ammon Hennacy and Ellen Thomas,** to a form of tax resistance in which they reduce their income below the tax threshold by taking up a simple living lifestyle. These individuals believe that their government is engaged in immoral, unethical or destructive activities such as war, and paying taxes inevitably funds these activities.

Art

The term **Bohemianism** has been used to describe a long tradition of both voluntary and involuntary poverty by artists who devote their time to artistic endeavors rather than paid labor.

In May 2014, a story on **NPR** suggested that positive attitudes towards living in poverty for the sake of art are becoming less common among young American artists, and quoted one recent graduate of the Rhode Island School of Design as saying "her classmates showed little interest in living in garrets and eating ramen noodles."

Economics

A new economics movement has been building since the UN conference on the environment in 1972, and the publication that year of Only One Earth, The Limits to Growth, and Blueprint for Survival, followed in 1973 by *Small Is Beautiful: Economics as If People Mattered.*

Recently, David Wann has introduced the idea of **"simple prosperity"** as it applies to a sustainable lifestyle. From his point of view, and as a point of departure for what he calls real sustainability, *"it is important to ask ourselves three fundamental questions: what is the point of all our commuting and consuming? What is the economy for? And, finally, why do we seem to be unhappier now than when we began our initial pursuit for rich abundance?"*

In this context, **simple living** is the opposite of our modern quest for affluence and, as a result, it becomes less preoccupied with quantity and more concerned about the preservation of cities, traditions and nature.

A reference point for this new economics can be found in James *Robertson's A New Economics of Sustainable Development,* and the work of thinkers and activists, who participate in his

Working for a Sane Alternative network and program. According to Robertson, the shift to sustainability is likely to require a widespread shift of emphasis from raising incomes to reducing costs.

The principles of the new economics, as set out by Robertson, are the following:

- systematic empowerment of people (as opposed to making and keeping them dependent), as the basis for people-centred development
- systematic conservation of resources and the environment, as the basis for environmentally sustainable development
- evolution from a "wealth of nations" model of economic life to a one-world model, and from today's inter-national economy to an ecologically sustainable, decentralising, multi-level one-world economic system
- restoration of political and ethical factors to a central place in economic life and thought
- respect for qualitative values, not just quantitative values.

One Thing You Can Do to fulfil this Chapter of your life.

Try to live your life like an open book whereas mastering what to bring out and what not to bring out. Being a little secretive is good. Try not to hold anything relevant back because I find that when you do that, you get stuck with negative things that simmer. It's better to let everything out there in art or late-night conversations that turn into early morning hugs. And when the vulnerability and imperfections spill out, you can pick them up off the floor in the early morning light and get a good look at them.

PART TWO:

The Revolution

Chapter 5 – Real Living.

"Be who you want to be, not what others want to see." ~Unknown

I made the decision to start living simply because I wanted fewer complications in my life but to struggle well.

Complications that revolved around:

- constantly agonizing over what to do with an overflowing wardrobe that was filled with impulse buys.

- an unhealthy relationship with food, which in turn, was destroying my relationship with my body.

- guilt from having a refrigerator that was always stuffed with expired food that I knew I had to eventually chuck into the bin.

- relationships that were bringing more drama and pain than love and support into my life.

- work that left me feeling numb and was becoming increasingly unfulfilling.

The combination of all these 'excesses' and unresolved dissatisfaction weighed heavily on my shoulders.

My life was starting to feel like a delicate plant whose branches were struggling to stay strong and upright amidst a storm that was threatening to snap every single one of them in half.

I wanted out of the storm, and into the calm. I wanted to feel lighter physically, mentally and emotionally.

I took questions that I'd been asking myself: Who did I want to become? What changes did I want to make to my life? Why did I *really* want to make them? When was the right time to make them? Where would I go?

But I had no answers, only more questions.

So, I decided to get the ball rolling by simplifying my life, freeing one weighed-down branch at a time, starting with my physical self. Exercising. Eating better. Then gradually, I moved on to my wardrobe, finances, and finally, the two most delicate branches of all: The relationships in my life, and my work.

SIMPLIFYING IS SIMPLE, BUT IT'S NOT WHAT YOU THINK, AND IT ISN'T EASY.

While my path to living a simpler life and letting go of everything that wasn't right for me helped bring more peace into my days, it also brought with it the pain of loss.

The loss of friendships, communities, and belief in both myself and others. There were times when I doubted myself for choosing the path that I did, when everyone else seemed to be scrambling to get ahead in the opposite direction.

While no one is a stranger to loss, I want to approach this conversation from a different angle: That loss isn't always a bad thing, and the truth is, simplifying your life *isn't* about shunning people, consumerism, money or material things. It's simply (pun intended) about embracing them in a more conscious, intentional way.

Well, at least for me it is, and you may decide to approach it differently with your own set of truths.

Some people call this way of living minimalism. I call it **simple living yet a life of greatness.**

But either way, if you're thinking of venturing down this still largely-unbeaten path, here are some ideas that I encourage you to consider folding into your practice, before you begin:

1. ALIGN YOUR ACTIONS WITH YOUR VALUES.

We may have goals that we want to achieve and values that we claim to live by, but often, our day-to-day actions fail to reflect them. But until your words, thoughts and actions align with each other, the values that you want to embody will remain dissociated from your reality as mere thoughts in your head.

2. SAY WHAT YOU MEAN, AND MEAN WHAT YOU SAY.

If you have a tendency to people-please like I do, it's all too easy to say "yes" when you really mean "no" or more specifically, "I don't want to". This can save the feelings of others from being hurt, but saying things you don't mean one too many times can eventually make you come across as inauthentic, and your trustworthiness, go *poof* in an instant.

3. PRIORITIZE MEANING OVER DOING.

You know the drill: Wake up, get dressed, go to work, have dinner, go to bed, repeat. Or on a macro level: Get born, go to school, go to college, get a boring job you hate but pays the bills, retire with regrets and then die. For many more, reality is much, much more terrifying and heart-breaking. If you're willing and able, why not **choose yourself** so that you *don't* have to live unconsciously on autopilot or in pain?

4. EAT FOODS YOU LOVE, BUT SET BOUNDARIES WITH THEM.

For years, I struggled with emotional eating and because of it, my weight. And after trying to 'fix' these imbalances with over-exercising and restrictive dieting—neither of which worked—I realized that the only way to find my way back to 'normal' eating was to heal my relationship with the food. My starting point? Figuring out why I was compulsively overeating, the triggers that led to it, and breaking the chain that led one to the other. With constant practice, I was able to eat the foods I love without going overboard, and in the process, lose all the extra weight I'd been carrying around for over two decades.

5. BE LESS IMPULSIVE AND MORE INTENTIONAL.

We're bombarded with thousands of ads every single day that encourage us to act impulsively on urges that bring us little to no real benefit. *"Feeling down? We've got the perfect outfit pick-me-up!"*. Or, *"That color looks AMAZING on you. You should really get it before it runs out"*. And I bought into them, over and over again until I realized that I was drowning in stuff that I never used, and a body weight that crushed my self-esteem.

6. BE LESS REACTIVE AND MORE RESPONSIVE.

Everyone has an ego, and most of us start out in life not knowing how to keep it in check. So, we throw tantrums. We yell. We bully. We make sure that we *always* have the last word. We make damn sure they know who's boss. We make sure that we're always right. Because we ARE right. Right? Not if you're intentionally hurting someone else or chipping away at your personal and professional relationships, one ego trip at a time.

7. VALUE KNOWLEDGE AND EXPERIENCES MORE THAN THINGS.

Having nice things is well, nice. But ultimately, the people who truly care about you don't care about the things you have. All they care about is that you're happy, and that you're able to spend time with them. And the people you're trying to impress with the nice things? They couldn't care less about whether you're happy or miserable, so why not choose to invest your time, energy and money in making beautiful memories with the ones who **do matter**, and knowledge that will help enrich your relationships with them?

The more experiences I have in life, the clearer it becomes to me that to be happy, the more discerning I need to be with how I spend my time, energy and money.

How do I do this? My gut always points me back to the same answer: Living a simple life.

If you're wondering if living a simple life is for you, here are 5 helpful resources that have made the biggest impact on my simple-living journey—resources that distill the true essence of living a meaningful, intentional life better than I ever could:

1. Minimalism: A Documentary About the Important Things, Joshua Fields Millburn and Ryan Nicodemus

If you're a brand-new to minimalism, this documentary is the perfect way to start off your journey. It takes you inside the minimalist worlds of Joshua Fields Millburn and Ryan Nicodemus, known collectively as The Minimalists, the painful circumstances that led them to this way of life, and the inspiring lives of others from different backgrounds who are doing the same.

2. The More of Less: Finding the Life You Want Under Everything You Own, Joshua Becker

Feeling intimidated by the thought of becoming a 'minimalist'? Joshua Becker unpacks the concept for you, one bit-sized idea at a time, helping you create a personal approach to getting rid of the clutter in your life to make room for what you truly want. This read isn't just about how get rid of overwhelm by living with fewer things, it's also about how to live your best life.

3. Soulful Simplicity: How Living with Less Can Lead to So Much More, Courtney Carver

Living a simple, minimalist life doesn't revolve around throwing out all your stuff or decluttering your home, and Courney Carver makes this refreshingly clear in her heart-centered memoir/how-to. In it, she encourages you to first figure out why you're considering simplifying your life, starting with a deeply touching account of how she discovered her own 'big why's' and the health crisis that led up to it.

4. Ikigai: The Japanese Secret to A Long and Happy Life, Héctor García and Francesca Miralles

This isn't a book that addresses simple living explicitly, but its goal, using the Japanese concept of ikigai (which when translated, means 'reason for being'), is the same: To achieve a happier, healthier and meaningful life. The inspiring setting that the authors use to demonstrate the principles they teach in this book? Okinawa, where the highest concentration of centenarians in the world live.

5. The Life-Changing Magic of Tidying Up: The Japanese Art of Decluttering and Organizing, Marie Kondo

If you've got stuff in your life, you need to read this book. Chapter by chapter, Marie Kondo teaches you how to whittle your belongings down to the items that bring you joy, as well as organize them in a way that honors their purpose in your life and keeps your home clutter-free.

If you haven't yet started simplifying your life, or just started to, know this: Living a simple life doesn't have to be about depriving yourself of things that bring you fulfilment and joy.

In fact, it's up to you to define what fulfilment and joy mean to you.

Once you do, it's time to lighten the heavy branches of your life, one leaf at a time.

Contributor of Huffington Post, Tom Casano, CEO and Founder of www.lifecoachspotter.com writes that: *A big house or a new car won't actually make you happier; it's the simple joys in life that bring true happiness.*

He distils further saying;

"Happiness is the meaning and the purpose of life, the whole aim and end of human existence."

Aristotle said this more than 2,000 years ago. And it still holds true today. What is the true purpose of life, if not to live a happy life until we die?

Happiness is one of the most sought-after goals in life, yet for many it seems to be elusive. It's easy to delude ourselves into thinking, "When I just have that nice house and new car, then I can be happy." But in reality, happiness is available to all of us, right now. A big house or a new car won't actually make you happier; it's the simple joys in life that bring true happiness. Read on to learn 15 simple ways that you can start living a happier life today.

1. Do What You Love
If your passion is playing soccer, writing poems, or teaching children how to swim, make time to do it. You'll find that when you're doing what you love, you're filled with joy. How much better does that sound than forcing yourself do something you don't like?

2. Help Others
Sometimes after we've achieved our own personal goals, we still feel empty inside because we haven't made a meaningful contribution to someone else's life. When we volunteer or help others, it feels good to just be of service to someone else. The impact we make feels fulfilling and is a big potential source for our own happiness.

3. Be Thankful
When you think of all the things that you have to be grateful for, you realize how blessed you already are. Without even realizing it, we take our basic necessities for granted -- a roof over your head and plenty of food to eat. By appreciating the things that you already have, you'll begin to feel happier in your life.

4. Share with Others

When we share our thoughts, our time, and our abilities with others we feel better for it. A life lived without sharing can become lonely. When you share with others, they'll feel great towards you and help you to feel more joy in your own life.

5. Smile More

Practice smiling more and see how it affects you internally, as well as those around you. You can always afford to give a smile. Smiling more makes you feel happier.

6. Exercise

When was the last time you went to the gym or worked out? Exercise reduces stress and releases endorphins, also known as a "runner's high." Playing sports is a fun way to exercise as well, whether it's kicking around a soccer ball or shooting hoops.

7. Seek Out a Life Coach

A life coach will help you to evaluate your life and why you're not feeling happy in it. Maybe you're holding limiting beliefs or you have an emotional block without realizing it. By speaking to a life coach, you can uncover why you're actually unhappy and what you can do to feel better.

8. Find Ways to Manage Stress

Don't let stress rob you of your birth right to be happy. You deserve to be happy, and it wouldn't be right to let stress get in the way. Practices such as meditation can help you to manage stress better and feel great.

9. Eat Healthy

I can't stress much on this - It's much more challenging to feel truly happy when you're sick. But when you eat right, you feel better both physically and mentally. And you'll avoid that guilty feeling that you just pigged out on junk food.

10. Spend Time with Your Loved Ones

There's no replacement for spending quality time with your loved ones. We're social beings, even if you're an introvert or a loner. People love spending time with their friends and family for good conversation, bonding, and some laughs. Life's too short to live it completely alone.

11. Dump Negative Thinking
You already know that negative thinking will bring you down. So how do you stop it? Become more aware of it and try replacing your negative thoughts with some positive ones. Spend less time with negative people and more time with positive people.

12. Give More Gifts
You don't have to give expensive gifts; sometimes a poem, a quick note, or a thoughtful email will brighten someone else's day, and yours. Share what you can give to all the wonderful people in your life.

13. Forgive and Forget
Holding a grudge will harm you more than the person you're holding it against. Ask yourself, "What would it take for me to let go of the past?" and notice how you feel when you let go of your anger for a few seconds. Focus instead on a bright future and you'll feel better for it.

14. Take a Walk in Nature
Spending time out in nature can be very refreshing and renewing, especially when you're living in an artificial, manmade world. Taking a walk in your local woods or park and getting some fresh air can allow you to appreciate the beauty of the natural world.

15. Be Yourself
As Steve Jobs said, "Your time is limited, so don't waste it living someone else's life." Accept who you are, just be yourself, and you'll feel a world of difference.

Today, we have access to all sorts of gadgets and apps that are supposed to make our lives easier, but ironically, all of these modern technologies only complicate life even more! So, how can we live a simple life in a fast-paced, complex world?

Well, we've come up with a list to help you do just that. Of course, you may not be able to (or want to) do all 101, but if you can pick at least 5 out of this list, you're off to a great start. Some of these things may be repeated because *Faith comes by hearing and hearing* which will stipulate you to action.

HERE ARE 101 WAYS YOU CAN START TO LIVE A SIMPLE LIFE, STARTING NOW:

1. Don't spend money on things you don't really need.

2. Avoid debts, if at all possible.

3. Have a garage sale to get rid of old junk you don't use.

4. Buy a bike instead of a car (you'll save money on insurance, gas, repairs, a car note, and maintenance).

5. Avoid costly medical bills by adopting a whole food, plant-based diet.

6. Prep meals for the week ahead of time.

7. Make your own beauty and hygiene products at home.

8. Make your own cleaning products (you'll avoid harmful chemicals and spend less).

9. Only keep the clothes you actually wear, and give away the rest.

10. Live in a smaller home

11. (If you're really feeling up to it) Live off-the-grid (or get grid-adjacent) to reduce or get rid of electric, gas, and water bills.

12. Start a garden, compost your food, and cut down on your weekly grocery bill.

13. Every time you buy something new, get rid of something old.

14. Have designated days to do laundry.

15. Drop your cell phone plan, and use the Wi-Fi in your home or Internet cafes instead.

16. Live closer to nature.

17. Buy a fluoride filter for your entire house so you don't have to buy jugs on non-fluoridated water.

18. Live within your means and adapt as you grow in wealth.

19. Adopt an attitude of gratitude.

20. Smile like you mean it. ☺

21. Avoid drama.

22. Unplug everything when you're not using it.

23. Have a set time each day to check social media (and stick to it).

24. Cancel your cable bill if you rarely watch TV.

25. Spend time outdoors as much as possible.

26. Let go of the past, and live in the present.

27. Create your future, but don't worry about what's to come.

28. Meditate daily.

29. Exercise often.

30. Try to use natural remedies for ailments when possible.

31. Give items you don't use to the homeless or poor.

32. Don't leave lights on when you're not home.

33. Try to buy energy-efficient appliances.

34. Buy high-quality items that won't need replacing often.

35. Automate your bill payments.

36. Reduce credit cards.

37. Don't charge anything you can't pay back quickly.

38. Listen more than you talk.

39. PLAY MORE!!!

40. Work less. ☺

41. Laugh at least 30 times a day.

42. Take relaxing baths in Epsom salt and lavender oil.

43. Have friends who inspire you.

44. Distance yourself from energy vampires.

45. Write down your goals, and go after them.

46. Don't wait for things to happen; make them happen.

47. Pack what you need for a flight in a carry-on bag only to avoid baggage fees.

48. Consider buying a used car instead of new.

49. Downsize when you can.

50. Become a warrior, not a worrier.

51. Turn your passion into your job.

52. See if you can work from home if possible.

53. Don't overbook your life.

54. Spend at least one day a week entirely in nature.

55. Speak gently to people.

56. Make your own dog or cat food for pets (cheaper and healthier).

57. Buy locally grown produce.

58. Only buy new things when old things break.

59. Shred old papers you don't need.

60. Avoid letting your emails pile up.

61. Organize your computer files.

62. Limit your time on social media.

63. Go with the flow.

64. Tackle problems before they get out of hand.

65. Say what you mean, and mean what you say.

66. Don't chase perfection; embrace imperfections.

67. Have a home gym to avoid paying for a gym membership.

68. Or, make nature your gym. ☺

69. Make to-do lists.

70. Simply SMILE.

71. Forgive and forget.

72. Make your own baby food if you have young children.

73. Let your kids play in nature (it's free) rather than buying them tons of toys.

74. Move to another country where the cost of living is cheaper.

75. Try to eliminate bills where you can.

76. Buy bundled services (phone and internet).

77. Check emails only a couple times a day.

78. Pack minimally for trips.

79. Eat at home more.

80. Wash dishes right after you eat so they don't pile up.

81. Love everyone.

82. Do all your errands in one go.

83. Buy clothing that will last.

84. Make a grocery list before you go shopping.

85. Have only a couple of email addresses.

86. Always tell the truth.

87. Follow your heart.

88. Appreciate the little things in life.

89. Practice positive thinking!

90. Give up alcohol and cigarettes (you'll save money and your health).

91. Wake up with the sun to get more done. ☺

92. Be productive.

93. Go to college only if you want to, not because you think you have to.

94. Become a self-taught learner, and seek information online.

95. Do what you enjoy, avoid what you don't.

96. Ask for help when you need it.

97. Delegate some chores to your kids or spouse.

98. Don't take on more work than you can do.

99. Stay humble.

100.   Keep an open mind.

101.   Carpool to reduce your carbon footprint and save money on gas.

Of course, these are not the only lessons you'll need for living a simple life. But the best ones are the ones you discover yourself. Try these and see what happens — I think you'll find out something beautiful about yourself, and about life.

The best kind of simplicity is that which exposes the raw beauty, joy and heartbreak of life as it is.

One Thing You Can Do to fulfil this Chapter of your life.

_____

Take an inventory of things which you will do which you believe would amount to a life which can serve as a model to someone to live a simple yet great one.

_____

Chapter 6 – Getting Ahead.

Let's be preposterous. Let's be ridiculous. Let's be utterly oblivious to what is expected of us. Let's change everything and really drop the jaws of bystanders. Let's break every rule not out of spite but out of necessity and dedication to the bigger picture.

- Mark Almond -

Let me tell you about what drives me. I wanted to stay up all night working on projects that I was proud of - projects that I was passionate about. And why shouldn't I be able to do these things? Why shouldn't YOU be able to do these things? This chapter is about staying true to ourselves. It is about loving who we are and what we're good at.

Do this and amazing things will happen for you.
If you want to blaze your own path you've got to be friends with the light and dark dangerous stuff inside you. The best metaphor I can think of to illustrate this is the example of white light passing through a prism. Unconditional love is like pure, white light. When you shine it through a prism, it refracts into all the different colors of the rainbow. These represent our emotions—joy, love, anxiety, envy, compassion, hate, empathy, and so on.

Each of us is like a prism, refracting pure white light (love) into all the different colors of the rainbow, and all of the hues (emotions) are equally needed for the whole. Few people, if any, would ever bring moral judgment against any given color. We wouldn't say, "Oh, that color is evil," or "That color is sinful." But we do this to people and their expressions of emotion, seeing some feelings as right and others as wrong.

When we judge some of our emotions as being negative and try to deny them, we're suppressing part of who we are. This creates a blockage within us and prevents us from expressing the fullness of our magnificence, just as extracting certain colors from the spectrum on the basis of a moral judgment would truncate the light and make it something it really isn't.

We don't have to act on every emotion; we just have to accept that they're part of who we are. Denying them would be like prohibiting a certain color from being refracted through the prism. Only by embracing the full spectrum of our feelings without judgment, can we get in touch with the pure essence of unconditional love that resides at our core

You've got to be friends with your emotions and know when to back off and when to fight through. You will get to know your inner self intimately. This happens when you face difficulties and problems and adversity in the external world. Eventually, the only thing left holding you back is yourself.

Failure just means you stop when things aren't going well. Success means finding a way to sustain, grow, or evolve. Birds can fly because they have hollow bones. Fish can swim because their gills absorb the oxygen from water. Artists can sleep late in the mornings because they learned when to compromise and when to stay the course. Believe it or not, it is actually hard work being ourselves. We've got teachers and parents and employers and neighbors and important community members barking at us like tiny terriers. A closer look will reveal their expectations as nothing but a vague set of reasonless rules. Regardless of what started the cycle, we have the power. We can take a stand and explain that we will do what makes us happy. And that will be the end of it. They can accept us for who we are or they can leave. If you can find the peace and clarity to accept where you are, you will soon have the insight to get where you'd like to go.

You've got people all around you explaining the rules and giving advice. They have many tiny suggestions. But what no one ever mentions is that sometimes trying something stupid can have the most extraordinary results. The days we ignore common sense are sometimes the days we can look back on when we're older and say, "Thank God I was bold that day."

They tell us that we'll never amount to anything. They tell us to go back to college. Get that MBA. They insist that if we don't learn how to dress properly, no one will ever take us seriously. They dribble red wine on the floor and they spit when they talk. The last time they saw a sunset, it was by happenstance on the way to a work meeting. The last time they felt any passion in the bedroom was when they drank too much at the country club. When they look in the mirror, they don't see themselves. They only see an image to be groomed by the standards of others. They have plenty of advice. And they're quite happy to share it. Sometimes it's okay to get angry. It's okay to stand on your own two feet and say to the world, "You're gonna have to accept me because I'm not leaving." Sometimes it's fine to shout out loud, let everybody know where you are and what you're thinking. Sometimes we've got no choice but to flaunt our stuff and show the world what we got.

Do you know how rare it is to be human?

Do you know what a miracle it is to get all your energy wrapped up in that functioning body of yours? It'd take 30 lifetimes just to understand it all. You are a walking, talking, embodiment of the consciousness of our planet and your only job is to love. Love yourself and love the people around you. Love the air you breathe and love every person you ever meet – whether they appreciate it or not. That stuff has transforming powers and it is a double-edged sword of helpfulness. It will change your life and elevate the people around you. The world doesn't want the same thing all of the time. They want something different. They want something honest and new. Don't cheapen yourself. Stay weird. If things feel boring or stale, do something unexpected. Continue to reinvent yourself and strive towards the extraordinary. Inner values are there for you when everything else falls apart. If you're well centered and true to who you are, you'll be able to make helpful compromises in the external world and build some extraordinary things with amazing people.

People who change the world don't get wrapped up in today's fashions.

It's your mind. You can believe in God or physics or love at first sight. You can believe in telepathy or prayer or astral projection. No one around you knows anymore about these things than you do. Try different things and see what works. For me, I vibe for my **Ultimate Father (God) in Heaven.**

What makes you feel good? What feels right? Forget the experts. They used to think the earth was flat. If you think you can communicate with loved ones who have died or control your own future by maintaining a positive attitude, then you are absolutely correct. When people tell you, you love somebody too much, don't listen to them. When they tell you to forget about it, don't listen to them. When they tell you to let him or her go, try harder to win him or her back. If you love someone, there's a reason. These things aren't just "in your head." The urges are real. Your feelings are real.

Be the calm, centered version of yourself. This is the most productive and inspiring version.

In school they teach us all to go after the same things. They teach us how to apply for the same jobs and how to compete with each other. In school, they teach us to avoid making mistakes. But mistakes are honest and mistakes are beautiful and mistakes are where insight comes from. What they never teach us in school is that the biggest rewards come from the biggest risks. If millions of people go to a top tier University to get their master's degree, the value of said degree decreases. If hundreds of people apply for the same job, the employer is in a position to lower salaries and cut benefits. When you play by the rules, you will always be in second place to the rule makers. In this day and age, we must burn our own paths. We must find a creative solution and be honest with what we're capable of accomplishing. It takes a mindset that is okay with fumbling around and learning how to be a leader. It takes someone who understands that taking risks is the only way to accomplish something great.

Don't be afraid to disregard that which does not get your blood boiling in the morning.

There is no need to imitate what is popular. We are all different for a reason. When we push our inner thoughts aside in hopes of winning approval – we lose touch with ourselves. There's no reason for it. We have plenty to offer just the way we are. Embrace risk and wonderful things will happen.

If you have a dream, if you have a love or a talent you want to perfect - you've got to be in charge of yourself. You can't look to others for direction or approval. No one cares. If you want to build the life you envision, you've got to have a lot of guts to go out there and do it your way. It takes years of practice, but if you're honest with yourself when challenges arise, you'll find the power to rise above. I think it's important for every person to have some sort of creative outlet to express themselves - especially those who aren't so good at holding a conversation. Writing works for me but try anything - hiking, podcasting, cooking or fly-fishing. If you can make a living from your creative endeavors, that is great but by no means necessary.

Don't let advertising agencies sell you the idea that you need something outside yourself to better your life. You are a miracle. Breaking the rules can sometimes turn out really well.

I believe in lifestyle design. I believe
in embracing passions and focusing on the things we're good at. I'm all about accepting ourselves and being honest about what we want. So, if I want to write books all night, I should be able to find a way to do that. If you want to throw out your cell phone and go live off the land, you should be able to go and do that. If you want to drop out of school and start a website about collecting vintage Zippos and spend your time restoring wicks and flints, what's stopping you?

Avoid those who always have comments or a critique about art or beauty or performance of any kind. Beware of people who are always talking. They lack wisdom and tend to miss the important things in life. Trust your gut. When you have a thought, don't push it aside. Listen to your intuition. And most importantly, when you think you are in love, you are. Be unapologetic. And you will come to know things about yourself that others only sometimes catch glimpses of while they doze off to sleep.

Art is personal and making art is selfish. You have to be selfish when you make art. If you're worried about what other people will think, you're going to lose the truth. You're going to break contact with the muse. It will all fall apart. When you are out and about and shaking hands in an art gallery, fine. Make eye contact and smile. Have meaningful discussions and be the 'relatable and friendly' version of yourself. But when you are in the honest flow of self-expression, there is no room for being polite. There is no room for anything but you and the force that put you here. Sometimes extraordinary and exciting new genres of music are invented by people on drugs who never learned how to properly play their instruments.

Appear where no one else can appear. Create things that no one has ever seen before. The secret to all of this is sustainability. Don't take a risk so big that you'll have to call it quits. Always have a way to stay in the game. The smartest thing you can do with a record deal is to take the advance and build a studio in your basement. That way, if the first record doesn't do well and you get dropped, you'll still have a studio in your basement to record the next one.

One of the worst feelings is to not have enough money in the bank to go out and start a new project. That's why I cook at home more often than eating out. It's why I only own some highly valuable pair of shoes and do not have cable television. I read a book recently in which the author argued that most people never become rich because they get bored too quickly. He claims that it takes years of patience and sacrifices to build wealth. It's imperative to stick to a financial plan. But most people get bored too quickly and move on to something else. They get distracted. They look for quick and easy solutions and fuck it up. I think the same thing is true for art or lifestyle creation. It's all about having an uncomplicated plan and having the endurance to show up every day and stick to the plan. You can't give up just because your first book didn't make the best-seller list.

The more you fail, the more capable you become. You might have heard

these trillion times as an advice. Here's a secret and this is a secret I believe with every ounce of my soul - If you don't succeed this time, you'll have double the chance of succeeding next time. I believe this to be true because when you are learning something new, you are figuring out how to finish it. You are making mistakes and learning how to avoid them next time. You're gaining insight on how to be more efficient with your efforts. Once you know how to do something once, you can do it again and again and get better every time.

Whatever it is that you're trying to do with your life, whether it's getting a gallery show in Chelsea or finding investor funds for a full-length feature film, keep hope. Keep your hope safe. Keep it safe in a jar and put some holes in the top so it can breathe. Hide it in a place where mom and dad will never find it. Remember to feed and water it daily. If someone asks to borrow it, refuse. Change your hiding place often and play with your hope every day. If you take care of your hope, it will get stronger. And it will grow and you will need a bigger jar. And one day, your hope won't fit in a jar anymore. Your hope will be too strong to ignore. It will grow like a hot air balloon. And you will not want to hide it anymore. When hope is ready, you will sail into the skies with it - shooting giant roars of flames that are so hot they'll take you where you've always wanted to go.

Change is good. It can turn your strengths into invincible powers. Sometimes you get sick of sitting in the chair so you build a standing desk. Sometimes you get bored with painting so you dive into sculpture. Whatever is happening in your world, don't stop. Things will click and doors will open. I believe in personal growth. But compromising for something you're not passionate about is not growth. Learning to wear a tie and sell blenders to the buyers of department stores is not growth.

How do you tell the difference between striving for growth and pretending to be something that you're not? Growth comes from facing fear. Pretending happens when you run from fear. Growth is something that comes after you do something that terrifies you. Pretending is when you never admit to yourself what you really wanted.

I think people should go after what they want in life because the things that scare us are damn tiny compared to that called death.

I am messy. And I am emotionally matured. I am flawed but I strive to be the best version of myself. I keep friends who accept every part of me and I do the same for them. I work in environments where I am allowed to shine. I love souls who are in tune with themselves and in love with the world. Audacity and passion will always mean more to me than the ability to emulate the talents of others.

Individual expression and niche marketing are the natural ways of the world. Cramming a one-size-fits-all product down people's throats makes most people want to throw up. Keep friends who inspire you - the ones who have your best interests at heart. Let go of those who bring you down. They will find other people to annoy.

If you feel like you're in last place, get out and start your own game. If you feel like you have a chance, try harder. And if you're in first place, continue to reinvent yourself. You make the rules. Everything you see around you can be changed.

WE DON'T HAVE TO ACTUALLY "WORK" AT

doing anything—like following specific rituals or dogma—to stay in touch with our magnificence. We can if we want to, if it brings us pleasure to do so, but it's not a requirement. Simply by following our internal guidance, we find what's right for us, including the methodology we use to look for it. We know we're on the right track when we feel ourselves at the center of our love without judgment of ourselves or others, and we recognize our true magnificence within the infinite Whole.

For example, prayer can bring great comfort to some people in times of need, and also for self-discovery. It may have a positive effect on well-being because of the process of letting go and handing over all burdens. As a result, people who pray may feel lighter and more uplifted, which contributes not only to their own well-being, but also to others since we're all connected. Any positivity you bring to yourself, you're bringing to the Whole.

However, I don't believe that those who pray are any more or less connected than those who don't. We all have our own way of recognizing that infinite space within us, and for some it may be prayer. For others, it can be music, art, being in nature, or even pursuing knowledge and technology—whatever brings out our passion, creativity and purpose for living. In other words, it's not prayer in and of itself that makes some of us more aware of our magnificence than others. Rather, it's choosing to conduct our lives by connecting with our own internal passion, bringing out a Zen-like quality and giving our lives meaning and a feeling of unity.

I personally don't feel the need to pray to an external god who's separate from me, because I know that I'm always One with the Universe, 100 percent of the time. Thus, I feel that my life is a prayer in itself. I do find meditation very helpful because it quiets my mind and helps me bring focus to that central point of awareness where I feel my connection with everything contained within the Whole. Meditation might not create this uplifting feeling for others, and that's fine. It's important to do what resonates on a personal level.

If you feel you can follow a system effortlessly, or if it's fun, that's great! But the minute it starts to be hard work or feel like a means of controlling your emotions or thoughts, it probably won't work very well for you. The state of pure allowing seems like the place where most positive change can occur. Let yourself be you, no matter who you are, embracing anything that makes you feel alive.

ALTHOUGH I STRONGLY BELIEVE

THAT the best thing, I can do for myself and others is to consciously keep myself uplifted and do what makes me feel happy, you may be surprised to learn that I don't advocate "positive thinking" as a blanket prescription. It's true that since all of life is connected, keeping myself in high spirits has a larger impact, as it is also what I'm putting out to the Whole.

However, if and when I notice negative thoughts creeping in, it seems best to allow them to pass through with acceptance and without judgment. When I try to suppress or force myself to change my feelings, the more I push them away, the more they push back. I just allow it all to flow through me, without judgment, and I find that the thoughts and emotions will pass. As a result, the right path for me unfolds in a totally natural way, letting me be who I truly am.

Sweeping statements such as "Negative

thoughts attracts negativity in life" aren't necessarily true, and can make people who are going through a challenging time feel even worse. It can also create fear that they're going to attract even more negativity with their thoughts. Using this idea indiscriminately often makes people going through seemingly tough times feel as though they're bad for attracting such events, and that's just not true. If we start to believe that it's our negative thoughts that are creating any unpleasant situations, we can become paranoid about what we're thinking. On the contrary, it actually has less to do with our thoughts than with our emotions, especially what we feel about ourselves.

It's also not the case that attracting positive things is simply about keeping upbeat. I can't say this strongly enough, but our feelings about ourselves are actually the most important barometer for determining the condition of our lives! In other words, being true to ourselves is more important than just trying to stay positive!

I allow myself to feel negatively about things that upset me because it's much better to experience real emotions than to bottle them up. Once again, it's about allowing what I'm actually feeling, rather than fighting against it. The very act of permitting without judgment is an act of self-love. This act of kindness toward myself goes much further in creating a joyful life than falsely pretending to feel optimistic.

Sometimes when we see someone who's really upbeat, effervescent, and kind, but whose life is crumbling, we may think, See? This "being positive" thing doesn't work. But here's the issue: we don't know that individual's inner dialogue. We don't know what other people are telling themselves day in and day out, or whether they're emotionally happy. And most important, we don't know whether they love and value themselves!

There are groups of seekers out there – natural born teachers offering guidance, passion and information. Find them. Embrace what you don't know and keep your ear to the ground. It's only when we realize that we don't know much, that we really start to grow. It takes guts to admit when you don't know something. It takes courage to reach out to someone and say, "I want to learn about what you do. Will you teach me?"

Keep people who inspire you in your life. Seek teachers and study great artists. No matter how talented or gifted you are, you've had a long line of great people come before you. Learn from them. I have many mentors. There will always be people who know more than me. There will always be people with more experience, more success, more money, maybe even more happiness. I find it best to know these people and to learn from them.

The best dividends on the labor invested have invariably come from seeking more knowledge rather than more power."

Signed Wilbur and Orville - Wright, March 12, 1906.

One Thing You Can Do to fulfil this Chapter of your life.

Getting ahead in life takes foresight and patience. Develop these traits and watch the world fall on you.

Chapter 7 — Being A Master

Everyone holds his fortune in his own hands, like a sculptor the raw material he will fashion into a figure. But it's the same with that type of artistic activity as with all others: We are merely born with the capability to do it. The skill to mold the material into what we want must be learned and attentively cultivated.
—JOHANN WOLFGANG VON GOETHE

There exists a form of power and intelligence that represents the high point of human potential. It is the source of the greatest achievements and discoveries in history. It is an intelligence that is not taught in our schools nor analysed by professors, but almost all of us, at some point, have had glimpses of it in our own experience. It often comes to us in a period of tension—facing a deadline, the urgent need to solve a problem, a crisis of sorts. Or it can come as the result of constant work on a project.

In any event, pressed by circumstances, we feel unusually energized and focused. Our minds become completely absorbed in the task before us. This intense concentration sparks all kinds of ideas—they come to us as we fall asleep, out of nowhere, as if springing from our unconscious. At these times, other people seem less resistant to our influence; perhaps we are more attentive to them, or we appear to have a special power that inspires their respect.

We might normally experience life in a passive mode, constantly reacting to this or that incident, but for these days or weeks we feel like we can determine events and make things happen.

We could express this power in the following way: Most of the time we live in an interior world of dreams, desires, and obsessive thoughts. But in this period of exceptional creativity, we are impelled by the need to get something done that has a practical effect.

We force ourselves to step outside our inner chamber of habitual thoughts and connect to the world, to other people, to reality.

Instead of flitting here and there in a state of perpetual distraction, our minds focus and penetrate to the core of something real. At these moments, it is as if our minds—turned outward—are now flooded with light from the world around us, and suddenly exposed to new details and ideas, we become more inspired and creative.

Once the deadline has passed or the crisis is over, this feeling of power and heightened creativity generally fades away. We return to our distracted state and the sense of control is gone. If only we could manufacture this feeling, or somehow keep it alive longer...but it seems so mysterious and elusive.

The problem we face is that this form of power and intelligence is either ignored as a subject of study or is surrounded by all kinds of myths and misconceptions, all of which only add to the mystery. We imagine that creativity and brilliance just appear out of nowhere, the fruit of natural talent, or perhaps of a good mood, or an alignment of the stars.

It would be an immense help to clear up the mystery—to name this feeling of power, to examine its roots, to define the kind of intelligence that leads to it, and to understand how it can be manufactured and maintained.

Let us call this sensation mastery—the feeling that we have a greater command of reality, other people, and ourselves. Although it might be something, we experience for only a short while, for others—Masters of their field—it becomes their way of life, their way of seeing the world.

(Such Masters include Leonardo da Vinci, Napoleon Bonaparte, Charles Darwin, Thomas Edison, and Martha Graham, among many others.) And at the root of this power is a simple process that leads to mastery—one that is accessible to all of us.

The process can be illustrated in the following manner: Let us say we are learning the piano, or entering a new job where we must acquire certain skills. In the beginning, we are outsiders. Our initial impressions of the piano or the work environment are based on prejudgments, and often contain an element of fear.

When we first study the piano, the keyboard looks rather intimidating—we don't understand the relationships between the keys, the chords, the pedals, and everything else that goes into creating music.

In a new job situation, we are ignorant of the power relationships between people, the psychology of our boss, the rules and procedures that are considered critical for success. We are confused—the knowledge we need in both cases is over our heads.

Although we might enter these situations with excitement about what we can learn or do with our new skills, we quickly realize how much hard work there is ahead of us. The great danger is that we give in to feelings of boredom, impatience, fear, and confusion. We stop observing and learning. The process comes to a halt.

If, on the other hand, we manage these emotions and allow time to take its course, something remarkable begins to take shape. As we continue to observe and follow the lead of others, we gain clarity, learning the rules and seeing how things work and fit together. If we keep practicing, we gain fluency; basic skills are mastered, allowing us to take on newer and more exciting challenges. We begin to see connections that were invisible to us before. We slowly gain confidence in our ability to solve problems or overcome weaknesses through sheer persistence.

At a certain point, we move from student to practitioner. We try out our own ideas, gaining valuable feedback in the process. We use our expanding knowledge in ways that are increasingly creative. Instead of just learning how others do things, we bring our own style and individuality into play.

As years go by and we remain faithful to this process, yet another leap takes place—to mastery. The keyboard is no longer something outside of us; it is internalized and becomes part of our nervous system, our fingertips. In our career, we now have a feel for the group dynamic, the current state of business. We can apply this feel to social situations, seeing deeper into other people and anticipating their reactions. We can make decisions that are rapid and highly creative. Ideas come to us. We have learned the rules so well that we can now be the ones to break or rewrite them.

In the process leading to this ultimate form of power, we can identify three distinct phases or levels.

The first is the Apprenticeship; the second is the Creative-Active; the third, Mastery. In the first phase, we stand on the outside of our field, learning as much as we can of the basic elements and rules.

We have only a partial picture of the field and so our powers are limited. In the second phase, through much practice and immersion, we see into the inside of the machinery, how things connect with one another, and thus gain a more comprehensive understanding of the subject.

With this comes a new power—the ability to experiment and creatively play with the elements involved. In the third phase, our degree of knowledge, experience, and focus is so deep that we can now see the whole picture with complete clarity. We have access to the heart of life—to human nature and natural phenomena.

That is why the artwork of Masters touches us to the core; the artist has captured something of the essence of reality. That is why the brilliant scientist can uncover a new law of physics, and the inventor or entrepreneur can hit upon something no one else has imagined.

We can call this power intuition, but intuition is nothing more than a sudden and immediate seizing of what is real, without the need for words or formulas.

The words and formulas may come later, but this flash of intuition is what ultimately brings us closer to reality, as our minds suddenly become illuminated by some particle of truth previously hidden to us and to others.

An animal has the capacity to learn, but it largely relies on its instincts to connect to its surroundings and save itself from danger.

Through instinct, it can act quickly and effectively. The human relies instead on thinking and rationality to understand its environment. But such thinking can be slow, and in its slowness can become ineffective.

So much of our obsessive, internal thought process tends to disconnect us from the world. Intuitive powers at the mastery level are a mix of the instinctive and the rational, the conscious and the unconscious, the human and the animal. It is our way of making sudden and powerful connections to the environment, to feeling or thinking inside things.

As children we had some of this intuitive power and spontaneity, but it is generally drummed out of us by all of the information that overloads our minds over time. Masters return to this childlike state, their works displaying degrees of spontaneity and access to the unconscious, but at a much higher level than the child.

If we move through the process to this endpoint, we activate the intuitive power latent in every human brain, one that we may have briefly experienced when we worked so deeply on a single problem or project. In fact, often in life we have glimpses of this power—for instance, when we have an inkling of what will come next in a particular situation, or when the perfect answer to a problem comes to us out of nowhere. But these moments are ephemeral and not based on enough experience to make them repeatable.

When we reach mastery, this intuition is a power at our command, the fruit of working through the lengthier process. And because the world prizes creativity and this ability to uncover new aspects of reality, it brings us tremendous practical power as well.

Think of mastery in this way: Throughout history, men and women have felt trapped by the limitations of their consciousness, by their lack of contact with reality and the power to affect the world around them.

They have sought all kinds of shortcuts to this expanded consciousness and sense of control, in the form of magic rituals, trances, incantations, and drugs.

They have devoted their lives to alchemy, in search of the philosopher's stone—the elusive substance that transformed all matter into gold.

This hunger for the magical shortcut has survived to our day in the form of simple formulas for success, ancient secrets finally revealed in which a mere change of attitude will attract the right energy.

There is a grain of truth and practicality in all of these efforts—for instance, the emphasis in magic on deep focus. But in the end, all of this searching is centered on something that doesn't exist—the effortless path to practical power, the quick and easy solution, the El Dorado of the mind.

At the same time that so many people lose themselves in these endless fantasies, they ignore the one real power that they actually possess.

 And unlike magic or simplistic formulas, we can see the material effects of this power in history—the great discoveries and inventions, the magnificent buildings and works of art, the technological prowess we possess, all works of the masterful mind.

This power brings to those who possess it the kind of connection to reality and the ability to alter the world that the mystics and magicians of the past could only dream of.

Over the centuries, people have placed a wall around such mastery. They have called it genius and have thought of it as inaccessible. They have seen it as the product of privilege, inborn talent, or just the right alignment of the stars. They have made it seem as if it were as elusive as magic. But that wall is imaginary. This is the real secret: the brain that we possess is the work of six million years of development, and more than anything else, this evolution of the brain was designed to lead us to mastery, the latent power within us all.

SPIRALS OF MASTERY

For three million years we were hunter-gatherers, and it was through the evolutionary pressures of that way of life that a brain so adaptable and creative eventually emerged. Today we stand with the brains of hunter-gatherers in our heads.

—RICHARD LEAKEY

It is hard for us to imagine now, but our earliest human ancestors who ventured out onto the grasslands of East Africa some six million years ago were remarkably weak and vulnerable creatures. They stood less than five feet tall. They walked upright and could run on their two legs, but nowhere near as fast as the swift predators on four legs that pursued them.

They were skinny—their arms could not provide much defense. They had no claws or fangs or poison to resort to if under attack. To gather fruits, nuts, and insects, or to scavenge dead meat, they had to move out into the open savanna where they became easy prey to leopards or packs of hyenas. So weak and small in number, they might have easily become extinct.

And yet within the space of a few million years (remarkably short on the time scale of evolution), these rather physically unimpressive ancestors of ours transformed themselves into the most formidable hunters on the planet. What could possibly account for such a miraculous turnaround?

Some have speculated that it was their standing on two legs, which freed up the hands to make tools with their opposable thumbs and precision grip. But such physical explanations miss the point.

Our dominance, our mastery does not stem from our hands but from our brains, from our fashioning the mind into the most powerful instrument known in nature—far more powerful than any claw. And at the root of this mental transformation are two simple biological traits—the visual and the social—that primitive humans leveraged into power.

Our earliest ancestors were descended from primates who thrived for millions of years in a treetop environment, and who in the process had evolved one of the most remarkable visual systems in nature. To move quickly and efficiently in such a world, they developed extremely sophisticated eye and muscle coordination.

Their eyes slowly evolved into a full-frontal position on the face, giving them binocular, stereoscopic vision. This system provides the brain a highly accurate three-dimensional and detailed perspective, but is rather narrow.

Animals that possess such vision—as opposed to eyes on the side or half side—are generally efficient predators like owls or cats. They use this powerful sight to home in on prey in the distance. Tree-living primates evolved this vision for a different purpose—to navigate branches, and to spot fruits, berries, and insects with greater effectiveness. They also evolved elaborate color vision.

When our earliest human ancestors left the trees and moved to the open grasslands of the savanna, they adopted an upright stance. Possessing already this powerful visual system, they could see far into the distance (giraffes and elephants might stand taller, but their eyes are on the sides, giving them instead panoramic vision).

This allowed them to spot dangerous predators far away on the horizon and detect their movements even in twilight. Given a few seconds or minutes, they could plot a safe retreat.

At the same time, if they focused on what was nearest at hand, they could identify all kinds of important details in their environment—footprints and signs of passing predators, or the colors and shapes of rocks that they could pick up and perhaps use as tools.

In the treetops, this powerful vision was built for speed—seeing and reacting quickly.

On the open grassland, it was the opposite. Safety and finding food relied upon slow, patient observation of the environment, on the ability to pick out details and focus on what they might mean. Our ancestors' survival depended on the intensity of their attention.

The longer and harder they looked, the more they could distinguish between an opportunity and a danger. If they simply scanned the horizon quickly, they could see a lot more, but this would overload the mind with information—too many details for such sharp vision.

The human visual system is not built for scanning, as a cow's is, but for depth of focus.

Animals are locked in a perpetual present. They can learn from recent events, but they are easily distracted by what is in front of their eyes.

Slowly, over a great period of time, our ancestors overcame this basic animal weakness. By looking long enough at any object and refusing to be distracted—even for a few seconds—they could momentarily detach themselves from their immediate surroundings.

In this way they could notice patterns, make generalizations, and think ahead. They had the mental distance to think and reflect, even on the smallest scale.

These early humans evolved the ability to detach and think as their primary advantage in the struggle to avoid predators and find food. It connected them to a reality other animal could not access.

Thinking on this level was the single greatest turning point in all of evolution—the emergence of the conscious, reasoning mind.

The second biological advantage is subtler, but equally powerful in its implications. All primates are essentially social creatures, but because of their intense vulnerability in open areas, our earliest ancestors had a much greater need for group cohesion. They depended on the group for vigilant observation of predators and the gathering of food. In general, these early hominids had many more social interactions than other primates.

Over the course of hundreds of thousands of years, this social intelligence became increasingly sophisticated, allowing these ancestors to cooperate with one another on a high level. And as with our understanding of the natural environment, this intelligence depended on deep attention and focus. Misreading the social signs in a tight-knit group could prove highly dangerous.

Through the elaboration of these two traits—the visual and the social—our primitive ancestors were able to invent and develop the complex skill of hunting some two to three million years ago. Slowly, they became more creative, refining this complex skill into an art.

They became seasonal hunters and spread throughout the Euro-Asian landmass, managing to adapt themselves to all kinds of climates. And in the process of this rapid evolution, their brains grew to virtually modern human size, some 200,000 years ago.

In the 1990s a group of Italian neuroscientists discovered something that could help explain this increasing hunting prowess of our primitive ancestors, and in turn something about mastery as it exists today. In studying the brains of monkeys, they found that particular motor-command neurons will not only fire when they execute a very specific action—such as pulling a lever to get a peanut or taking hold of a banana—but that these neurons will also fire when monkeys observe another performing the same actions. These were soon dubbed mirror neurons.

This neuronal firing meant that these primates would experience a similar sensation in both doing and observing the same deed, allowing them to put themselves in the place of another and perceive its movements as if they were doing them. It would account for the ability of many primates to imitate others, and for the pronounced abilities of chimpanzees to anticipate the plans and actions of a rival. Such neurons, it is speculated, evolved because of the social nature of primate life.

Recent experiments have demonstrated the existence of such neurons in humans, but on a much higher level of sophistication.

A monkey or primate can see an action from the point of view of the performer and imagine its intentions, but we can take this further. Without any visual cues or any action on the part of others, we can place ourselves inside their minds and imagine what they might be thinking.

For our ancestors, the elaboration of mirror neurons would allow them to read each other's desires from the subtlest of signs and thus elevate their social skills. It would also serve as a critical component in toolmaking—one could learn to fashion a tool by imitating the actions of an expert.

But perhaps most important of all, it would give them the ability to think inside everything around them. After years of studying particular animals, they could identify with and think like them, anticipating behavioural patterns and heightening their ability to track and kill prey. This thinking inside could be applied to the inorganic as well. In fashioning a stone tool, expert toolmakers would feel as one with their instruments.

The stone or wood they cut with became an extension of their hand. They could feel it as if it were their own flesh, permitting much greater control of the tools themselves, both in making and in using them.

This power of the mind could be unleashed only after years of experience. Having mastered a particular skill—tracking prey, fashioning a tool—it was now automatic, and so while practicing the skill the mind no longer had to focus on the specific actions involved but instead could concentrate on something higher— what the prey might be thinking, how the tool could be felt as part of the hand. This thinking inside would be a preverbal version of third-level intelligence—the primitive equivalent of Leonardo da Vinci's intuitive feel for anatomy and landscape or Michael Faraday's for electromagnetism. Mastery at this level meant our ancestors could make decisions rapidly and effectively, having gained a complete understanding of their environment and their prey. If this power had not evolved, the minds of our ancestors would have become easily overwhelmed by the mass of information they had to process for a successful hunt. They had developed this intuitive power hundreds of thousands of years before the invention of language, and that is why when we experience this intelligence it seems like something preverbal, a power that transcends our ability to put it into words.

Understand: This long stretch of time played a critical, elemental role in our mental development. It fundamentally altered our relationship to time. For animals, time is their great enemy. If they are potential prey, wandering too long in a space can spell instant death. If they are predators, waiting too long will only mean the escape of their prey. Time for them also represents physical decay. To a remarkable extent, our hunting ancestors reversed this process. The longer they spent observing something, the deeper their understanding and connection to reality. With experience, their hunting skills would progress. With continued practice, their ability to make effective tools would improve. The body could decay but the mind would continue to learn and adapt. Using time for such effect is the essential ingredient of mastery.

In fact, we can say that this revolutionary relationship to time fundamentally altered the human mind itself and gave it a particular quality or grain. When we take our time and focus in depth, when we trust that going through a process of months or years will bring us mastery, we work with the grain of this marvellous instrument that developed over so many millions of years. We infallibly move to higher and higher levels of intelligence. We see more deeply and realistically. We practice and make things with skill. We learn to think for ourselves. We become capable of handling complex situations without being overwhelmed. In following this path, we become Homo magister, man or woman the Master.

To the extent that we believe we can skip steps, avoid the process, magically gain power through political connections or easy formulas, or depend on our natural talents, we move against this grain and reverse our natural powers. We become slaves to time—as it passes, we grow weaker, less capable, trapped in some dead-end career. We become captive to the opinions and fears of others. Rather than the mind connecting us to reality, we become disconnected and locked in a narrow chamber of thought. The human that depended on focused attention for its survival now becomes the distracted scanning animal, unable to think in depth, yet unable to depend on instincts.

It is the height of stupidity to believe that in the course of your short life, your few decades of consciousness, you can somehow rewire the configurations of your brain through technology and wishful thinking, overcoming the effect of six million years of development. To go against the grain might bring temporary distraction, but time will mercilessly expose your weakness and impatience.

The great salvation for all of us is that we have inherited an instrument that is remarkably plastic. Our hunter-gatherer ancestors, over the course of time, managed to craft the brain into its present shape by creating a culture that could learn, change, and adapt to circumstances, that wasn't a prisoner to the incredibly slow march of natural evolution. As modern individuals, our brains have the same power, the same plasticity. At any moment we can choose to shift our relationship to time and work with the grain, knowing of its existence and power. With the element of time working for us, we can reverse the bad habits and passivity, and move up the ladder of intelligence.

Think of this shift as a return to your radical, deep past as a human, connecting to and maintaining a magnificent continuity with your hunter-gatherer ancestors in a modern form. The environment we operate in may be different, but the brain is essentially the same, and its power to learn, adapt, and master time is universal.

DOORS TO MASTERY

A man should learn to detect and watch that gleam of light which flashes across his mind from within, more than the luster of the firmament of bards and sages. Yet he dismisses without notice his thought, because it is his. In every work of genius, we recognize our own rejected thoughts; they come back to us with a certain alienated majesty.

—RALPH WALDO EMERSON

If all of us are born with an essentially similar brain, with more or less the same configuration and potential for mastery, why is it then that in history only a limited number of people seem to truly excel and realize this potential power? Certainly, in a practical sense, this is the most important question for us to answer.

The common explanations for a Mozart or a Leonardo da Vinci revolve around natural talent and brilliance. How else to account for their uncanny achievements except in terms of something they were born with? But thousands upon thousands of children display exceptional skill and talent in some field, yet relatively few of them ever amount to anything, whereas those who are less brilliant in their youth can often attain much more. Natural talent or a high IQ cannot explain future achievement.

As a classic example, compare the lives of Sir Francis Galton and his older cousin, Charles Darwin. By all accounts, Galton was a super-genius with an exceptionally high IQ, quite a bit higher than Darwin's (these are estimates done by experts' years after the invention of the measurement). Galton was a boy wonder who went on to have an illustrious scientific career, but he never quite mastered any of the fields he went into. He was notoriously restless, as is often the case with child prodigies.

Darwin, by contrast, is rightly celebrated as the superior scientist, one of the few who has forever changed our view of life. As Darwin himself admitted, he was "a very ordinary boy, rather below the common standard in intellect.... I have no great quickness of apprehension.... My power to follow a long and purely abstract train of thought is very limited." Darwin, however, must have possessed something that Galton lacked.

In many ways, a look at the early life of Darwin himself can supply an answer to this mystery. As a child Darwin had one overriding passion—collecting biological specimens. His father, a doctor, wanted him to follow in his footsteps and study medicine, enrolling him at the University of Edinburgh. Darwin did not take to this subject and was a mediocre student.

His father, despairing that his son would ever amount to anything, chose for him a career in the church. As Darwin was preparing for this, a former professor of his told him that the HMS Beagle was to leave port soon to sail around the world, and that it needed a ship's biologist to accompany the crew in order to collect specimens that could be sent back to England. Despite his father's protests, Darwin took the job. Something in him was drawn to the voyage.

Suddenly, his passion for collecting found its perfect outlet. In South America he could collect the most astounding array of specimens, as well as fossils and bones. He could connect his interest in the variety of life on the planet with something larger—major questions about the origins of species.

He poured all of his energy into this enterprise, accumulating so many specimens that a theory began to take shape in his mind. After five years at sea, he returned to England and devoted the rest of his life to the single task of elaborating his theory of evolution. In the process he had to deal with a tremendous amount of drudgery—for instance, eight years exclusively studying barnacles to establish his credentials as a biologist. He had to develop highly refined political and social skills to handle all the prejudice against such a theory in Victorian England. And what sustained him throughout this lengthy process was his intense love of and connection to the subject.

The basic elements of this story are repeated in the lives of all of the great Masters in history: a youthful passion or predilection, a chance encounter that allows them to discover how to apply it, an apprenticeship in which they come alive with energy and focus.

They excel by their ability to practice harder and move faster through the process, all of this stemming from the intensity of their desire to learn and from the deep connection they feel to their field of study. And at the core of this intensity of effort is in fact a quality that is genetic and inborn—not talent or brilliance, which is something that must be developed, but rather a deep and powerful inclination toward a particular subject.

This inclination is a reflection of a person's uniqueness. This uniqueness is not something merely poetic or philosophical—it is a scientific fact that genetically, every one of us is unique; our exact genetic makeup has never happened before and will never be repeated. This uniqueness is revealed to us through the preferences we innately feel for particular activities or subjects of study. Such inclinations can be toward music or mathematics, certain sports or games, solving puzzle-like problems, tinkering and building, or playing with words.

With those who stand out by their later mastery, they experience this inclination more deeply and clearly than others. They experience it as an inner calling. It tends to dominate their thoughts and dreams. They find their way, by accident or sheer effort, to a career path in which this inclination can flourish. This intense connection and desire allow them to withstand the pain of the process—the self-doubts, the tedious hours of practice and study, the inevitable setbacks, the endless barbs from the envious. They develop a resiliency and confidence that others lack.

In our culture we tend to equate thinking and intellectual powers with success and achievement. In many ways, however, it is an emotional quality that separates those who master a field from the many who simply work at a job. Our levels of desire, patience, persistence, and confidence end up playing a much larger role in success than sheer reasoning powers. Feeling motivated and energized, we can overcome almost anything. Feeling bored and restless, our minds shut off and we become increasingly passive.

In the past, only elites or those with an almost superhuman amount of energy and drive could pursue a career of their choice and master it. A man was born into the military, or groomed for the government, chosen among those of the right class. If he happened to display a talent and desire for such work it was mostly a coincidence. Millions of people who were not part of the right social class, gender, and ethnic group were rigidly excluded from the possibility of pursuing their calling. Even if people wanted to follow their inclinations, access to the information and knowledge pertaining to that particular field was controlled by elites. That is why there are relatively few Masters in the past and why they stand out so much.

These social and political barriers, however, have mostly disappeared. Today we have the kind of access to information and knowledge that past Masters could only dream about. Now more than ever, we have the capacity and freedom to move toward the inclination that all of us possess as part of our genetic uniqueness. It is time that the word "genius" becomes demystified and de-rarefied. We are all closer than we think to such intelligence. (The word "genius" comes from the Latin, and originally referred to a guardian spirit that watched over the birth of each person; it later came to refer to the innate qualities that make each person uniquely gifted.)

Although we may find ourselves at a historical moment rich in possibilities for mastery, in which more and more people can move toward their inclinations, we in fact face one last obstacle in attaining such power, one that is cultural and insidiously dangerous: The very concept of mastery has become denigrated, associated with something old-fashioned and even unpleasant. It is generally not seen as something to aspire to. This shift in value is rather recent, and can be traced to circumstances peculiar to our times.

We live in a world that seems increasingly beyond our control. Our livelihoods are at the whim of globalized forces. The problems that we face—economic, environmental, and so on—cannot be solved by our individual actions. Our politicians are distant and unresponsive to our desires. A natural response when people feel overwhelmed is to retreat into various forms of passivity. If we don't try too much in life, if we limit our circle of action, we can give ourselves the illusion of control. The less we attempt, the less chances of failure. If we can make it look like we are not really responsible for our fate, for what happens to us in life, then our apparent powerlessness is more palatable. For this reason, we become attracted to certain narratives: it is genetics that determines much of what we do; we are just products of our times; the individual is just a myth; human behavior can be reduced to statistical trends.

Many take this change in value a step further, giving their passivity a positive veneer. They romanticize the self-destructive artist who loses control of him-or herself. Anything that smacks of discipline or effort seems fussy and passé: what matters is the feeling behind the artwork, and any hint of craftsmanship or work violates this principle.

They come to accept things that are made cheaply and quickly. The idea that they might have to expend much effort to get what they want has been eroded by the proliferation of devices that do so much of the work for them, fostering the idea that they deserve all of this—that it is their inherent right to have and to consume what they want. "Why bother working for years to attain mastery when we can have so much power with very little effort? Technology will solve everything." This passivity has even assumed a moral stance: "mastery and power are evil; they are the domain of patriarchal elites who oppress us; power is inherently bad; better to opt out of the system altogether," or at least make it look that way.

If you are not careful, you will find this attitude infecting you in subtle ways. You will unconsciously lower your sights as to what you can accomplish in life. This can diminish your levels of effort and discipline below the point of effectiveness. Conforming to social norms, you will listen more to others than to your own voice. You may choose a career path based on what peers and parents tell you, or on what seems lucrative. If you lose contact with this inner calling, you can have some success in life, but eventually your lack of true desire catches up with you. Your work becomes mechanical. You come to live for leisure and immediate pleasures. In this way you become increasingly passive, and never move past the first phase. You may grow frustrated and depressed, never realizing that the source of it is your alienation from your own creative potential.

Before it is too late you must find your way to your inclination, exploiting the incredible opportunities of the age that you have been born into. Knowing the critical importance of desire and of your emotional connection to your work, which are the keys to mastery, you can in fact make the passivity of these times work in your favor and serve as a motivating device in two important ways.

First, you must see your attempt at attaining mastery as something extremely necessary and positive. The world is teeming with problems, many of them of our own creation. To solve them will require a tremendous amount of effort and creativity. Relying on genetics, technology, magic, or being nice and natural will not save us. We require the energy not only to address practical matters, but also to forge new institutions and orders that fit our changed circumstances.

We must create our own world or we will die from inaction. We need to find our way back to the concept of mastery that defined us as a species so many millions of years ago. This is not mastery for the purpose of dominating nature or other people, but for determining our fate. The passive ironic attitude is not cool or romantic, but pathetic and destructive. You are setting an example of what can be achieved as a Master in the modern world. You are contributing to the most important cause of all—the survival and prosperity of the human race, in a time of stagnation.

Second, you must convince yourself of the following: people get the mind and quality of brain that they deserve through their actions in life. Despite the popularity of genetic explanations for our behavior, recent discoveries in neuroscience are overturning long-held beliefs that the brain is genetically hardwired. Scientists are demonstrating the degree to which the brain is actually quite plastic—how our thoughts determine our mental landscape. They are exploring the relationship of willpower to physiology, how profoundly the mind can affect our health and functionality. It is possible that more and more will be discovered about how deeply we create the various patterns of our lives through certain mental operations—how we are truly responsible for so much of what happens to us.

People who are passive create a mental landscape that is rather barren. Because of their limited experiences and action, all kinds of connections in the brain die off from lack of use. Pushing against the passive trend of these times, you must work to see how far you can extend control of your circumstances and create the kind of mind you desire—not through drugs but through action. Unleashing the masterful mind within, you will be at the vanguard of those who are exploring the extended limits of human willpower.

In many ways, the movement from one level of intelligence to another can be considered as a kind of ritual of transformation. As you progress, old ideas and perspectives die off; as new powers are unleashed, you are initiated into higher levels of seeing the world. Consider Mastery as an invaluable tool in guiding you through this transformative process. Mastery helps lead you from the lowest levels to the highest. It will help to initiate you into the first step—discovering your Life's Task, or vocation, and how to carve out a path that will lead you to its fulfilment on various levels. It will advise you how to exploit to the fullest your apprenticeship—the various strategies of observation and learning that will serve you best in this phase; how to find the perfect mentors; how to decipher the unwritten codes on political behavior; how to cultivate social intelligence; and finally, how to recognize when it is time to leave the apprenticeship nest and strike out for yourself, entering the active, creative phase.

It will show you how to continue the learning process on a higher level. It will reveal timeless strategies for creative problem solving, for keeping your mind fluid and adaptable. It will show you how to access more unconscious and primitive layers of intelligence, and how to endure the inevitable barbs of envy that will come your way. It will spell out the powers that will come to you through mastery, pointing you in the direction of that intuitive, inside feel for your field. Finally, it will initiate you into a philosophy, a way of thinking that will make it easier to follow this path.

The structure of Mastery is simple yet great.

Excerpt from the *Book Mastery – By Robert Greene*

*In the book, **Robert Greene** dissects Mastery, at its core – not just mastery: He attributes mastery to patience and dedication instilling that no matter the number of years taken to ascertain a certain level of near perfection, it rises you to a great life.*

EXERCISE

1. What do you think being a Master in your calling or gift can render in your life?

....
....
....
....

2. List three things which upon mastering will give you a simple yet great life you envisioned.

....
....
....

3. What will you reflect on when you are in your death bed? Pain of Mastering a simple life or Regret of a cluttered and complex life and Why?.

....
....
....
....
....
....
....

One Thing You Can Do to fulfil this Chapter of your life.

---

*Embrace your calling, find the **One thing** you were born to do mastering it and let the rest follow.*

PART THREE:

PROACTIVE FUTURE

Chapter 8 – Having A long-term vision

---

20 years from now, you will be more disappointed by the things you didn't do by the things you did do so throw off the bow lines and explore your dreams.
—Unknown

A VISION is a precise, clearly defined goal with a detailed plan and timetable for achieving that goal.
Humanity is doomed if we fail to have vision for the future. In the beginning chapters of the Bible, The Lord becomes saddened because His people were perishing due to lack of;

- Vision
- Knowledge

This throws an unbending light that the progress of our lives can be powered with full force if we start to acknowledge the essence of vision. In this Chapter I will elaborate having not just a vision but a robust and a long-term vision. Vision is a term which is so much popularized by man but its tenets has not been taken into dual insight.

A simple yet great life can be attributed to this. Companies need this force and individuals need this force. When you look at all the wonderful and most admired brands or companies in the world, there is one thing which is irrefutable in the building process of their companies. This is a channel of a long-term vision the Founder or CEO has. Moreover, this vision has to be communicated to the customers, staff or employees of the company periodically to know where they are heading. Ability to see the future before it comes is an evidence of vision and faith.

No matter who you are or what country you live in, you have a personal purpose, for every human being is born with one. God created each person with a unique vision. He has tremendous plans for you that no one else can accomplish. The tragic thing is that many people live their whole lives without ever recognizing their visions. A lack of purpose and unfulfilled potential is epidemic in our world. Most people's lives do not reflect who they truly are or what they can be. Inside them are dreams that are not yet reality, gifts and talents they have not yet developed, purposes for their lives that are not yet fulfilled, the "something" they've always wanted to be or do but for some reason have not been able to accomplish.

Vision is a conception that is inspired by God in the heart of a human. The greatest gift God ever gave humanity is not sight, but vision. Sight is a function of the eyes, but vision is a function of the heart. You can have sight but no vision. *Throughout history, progress has been made only by people who have "seen" things that were not yet here. They were willing to be not right in their building of their vision(idealism) which lead to many failures but revolutionized the world.* Vision is seeing the future before it comes into being. It is a mental picture of your destiny. God gave humanity the gift of vision so we would not have to live only by what we see.

What have you always wanted to do? What is your heart's desire? What is your dream? When you can begin to see your vision clearly, you will be able to fulfil your life's purpose. The essence of vision is the ability to see farther than your physical eyes can look—to see not just what is, but also what can be and to make it a reality.

Consider this analogy: The destiny of an acorn is a tree. By faith, you can see the tree within the seed. You have a vision of it in your mind's eye because you know the potential in the seed. The same thing is true for you and me. God has given us birth for a purpose, and as far as God is concerned, that purpose is already finished because He has placed within us the potential for fulfilling it. We can see that purpose through faith.

To paraphrase the Bible, faith is the substance of things you hope to accomplish, the evidence of things you can see even when others cannot. Only by seeing what is not yet here can you bring something new, creative, and exciting into existence. Your dreams, talents, and desires can be refined in a process of discovering and fulfilling your vision so that your unique and personal gifts to this world will shine forth.

I believe with all my heart that when you have no vision, you will simply relive the past with its disappointments and failures. As long as a person has vision, however, there is always a chance for him to move out of his present circumstances and toward the fulfilment of his purpose. Therefore, vision is the key to your future.

This Chapter will help you to reassess your life's strategies and make the necessary adjustments so you can plan for the future and not make the same mistakes and decisions that have hindered you in the past. You will come to understand the principles of vision as well as the practical tools and skills necessary to bring your vision into reality.

CREATING A LONG-TERM VISION

Be like an eagle: An eagle is one of the most powerful creatures on the planet earth. The eagle is known for its distinct characteristics among all birds. Its known to be the king of the Air. Why? An eagle has an attitude which differentiates itself from all the animals. It thinks on a different level, it sees on a higher level, it flies on a higher level. It functions on another level. It loves on another level. It has a stronger vision than all the animals in the bird kingdom.

Now, when you begin to craft a long-term vision like an eagle, not only do you come to a point of realization knowing that you devised a flexible plan but it evolves and awakens you to the deep-seated talents, gifts and abilities you possess which you never knew were there or could use.
Grand visions go with grand rewards.

Now, take a sheet of paper or your journal and
Devise a long-range vision for
- 10 years to come
- 30 years to come
- 40 years to come
- 50 years to come.
- 100 years to come or even more for yourself or for your business/company.
- Or Generational Vision

  This vision must be foreseeing in areas of:
  - Health
  - Career
  - Finances
  - Dream
  - Relationships
  - Business
  - Lifestyle
  - Knowledge and Wisdom Bank
  - Four generations to come
  - Travelling Experiences, etc.

A wonderful vision plan devised by a company named **Softbank Corporation** gives a vivid light on this. They have come up with what they call A **300-year Vision Fund.** With this, **the founder, Masayoshi Son** aggressively went on hunt for funds from prominent corporations like Apple, Nvidia, The Prince of UAE and others to be invested which amounted to almost Hundred billion dollars ($100,000,000,000). This fund is known to be used for an incoming revolution which will spark many industries in the world like robots, Self-driving Cars, the use of the Suns solar energy as source of power, highly intelligent A.I etc.
This is the biggest vision I have ever heard from any company.

When you begin to envision like an eagle who sees from a height that a normal bird can't see, you must lock on your **target** with focus and go straight for it without compromise.

Lock on your target

Your target refers to what you intend to have in your life and for the next generation. Remember, we want to live a simple, yet great life. Locking on your target will be just like a missile given an exact location to hit.

Begin to think of things you would really want – I guarantee you that everything you want will streamline from great things – In the eyes of another, it might be opposite, so it's advisable you deduce these things by yourself.

It can be:
- Being with your family and providing unconditional love at all costs.
- Creating a powerful product.
- An idea sparked in the mind which can change millions of lives.
- Rendering an exceptional service.
- one room home which can be used by the next generation.
- A business tower/s which can serve as a family property in future.
- A company which will exists for more than 100 years
- A family which will be known for creating value or helping others, being selfless.
- Identified as being the source in the lives of others what which you want to experience.
- A family known for its distinct cultural imprint.
- A legacy / dent you want to leave on this earth / universe.
- Fulfilling your calling.

Since we are all different or unique human beings, we all have different thoughts as to what we believe it's simple for our liking which is genuine. So, go for what resonates with you deeply.

HAVE A GENERATIONAL VISION

A generational vision is a holistic vision created to announce the purpose of a group especially a family, providing unique imprint of a set of characteristics that will set millennials of that family to follow a track record which is indispensable.

You might not have your vision like that of Softbank Cooperation but thinking in a phase of generational-like can also help. As an individual, if your efforts are underlined based on a generational vision, it will ignite the framework of your family to also live a simple, yet great life because of what you want and intend to leave for the next generation even after your death.

A long-term vision for a family not only affects the unborn children but such families in rare cases leave great legacies.

I have personally devised such vision because looking back into my family's' tree, there seemed to be broken branches, as a result, I believe my generational vision will bring a new light and restructure my family which will affects every facets of the family including love, bonding , peace , abundance , sense of purpose , self-worth/self-esteem, passion, and greater heights of exploration.

Join me by coming up with a generational vision that will catapult both your business or life. It's time to stop the narrow thinking and come to the realization that there is a bigger world filled with discoveries, inventions, ideas, etc residing within you and me.

A family without a generational vision becomes a generational failure. Some do overcome the failure, some don't.

- Emmer -

One Thing You Can Do to fulfil this Chapter of your life.

*Carve a Long-**term Vision for your yourself, family and business**, taking a snapshot of how it will look like in the mind's eye.*

Chapter 9 – Mission Driven

Let us rid death of its strangeness, come to know it, get used to it. Let us have nothing on our minds as often as death. At every moment let us picture it in our imagination in all its aspects. . .. It is uncertain where death awaits us; let us await it everywhere. Premeditation of death is premeditation of freedom. . . . He who has learned how to die has unlearned how to be a slave. Knowing how to die frees us from all subjection and constraint.
—*Michel de Montaigne* —

Mission is our calling we all have but thoroughly distinct to each human being on this earth. Vision and mission go along together – When there is a vision, there is a mission to accomplish. Throughout history, people have set different courses in achieving what they believed were truly worthwhile.

They embraced a mission which lasted for years but went on to affect millions of people positively or negatively according to the purpose behind it.

We can all set a grand mission for ourselves in putting ourselves out there and achieving what is seemingly impossible before the human eyes. With that said, many of us unfortunately, are not mission driven thus purpose unfulfilled.

What can we do to stipulate a life which will shower forth a dexterity in future reflection which can lead us ultimately satisfied in the end? I can't stress much on this because at every living moment we are making conscious or unconscious choices as to whether we are embracing this mission or not. It's up to you.

I remember when I was in primary school writing a note which said '' What is my mission on this earth''. This question came as a result of a girl I really liked and almost fell in love with. She was by the name Abigail. Well, Abigail was very notorious as I try as much as possible to get closer. She would always ignore or pretend as if I was absent. I think my childish play lead me to writing that question which really sparked curiosity within me. The question that I threw then was to understand why I was so attached to this girl even though she didn't like me. I continued to understand with time that the urge I had was to let me understand that I had a part to play in this girl's life.

A mission driven life is crucial to understanding and moving towards a life you never thought would lead you to. A mission driven life knows the why, How and What behind it. In Simon Sinek's book *Find your Why*, he helps us to understand our mission through asking ourselves these three questions beginners – Why, What and How, related to us as individuals or companies.

THE GOLDEN CIRCLE

The Golden Circle is a concept described by Simon; it shows how certain leaders have the ability to inspire action rather than simply manipulating people to act. Simon emphasises that the majority of leaders however, choose manipulation over inspiration when it comes to motivating followers.

Simon uses three tiers to differentiate between companies and their motivations; **What, How & Why**.

Every company in the world knows **WHAT they do** -e.g. they can describe and define their product or service. Some companies know **HOW they do** what they do -e.g. they know that their unique selling point is the reason they stand out. Very few companies know **WHY they do what they do** (and it's not to make money, this is a result). Why do you get out of bed in the morning, what is the companies' purpose, and why should anyone care?

Simon uses Apple as the example of an inspirational company. The format a normal company would use to communicate their product goes like this; 'this is what we do, and this is how we do it.' However, inspiring companies such as Apple start with why, they reverse the order of information, e.g.;

WHY - In everything that we do, we believe in challenging the status quo and thinking differently. (This part engages the consumer on an emotional level.)

HOW - The way we do this is to design products that are beautifully designed and easy to use. (The how and the what serve as evidence of the why.)

WHAT - We just so happen to make great computers. Wanna buy one?" *It's not a debate about better or worse anymore, it's a discussion about different needs. And before the discussion can even happen, the WHYs for each must be established first."*

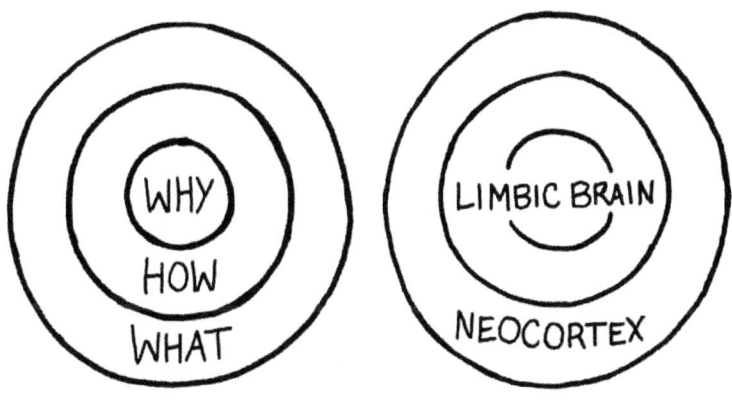

Image Credit: Simon Sinek - *Start with Why: How Great Leaders Inspire Everyone to Take Action*

This is Biology

When a company starts with what, there is likely going to be some appeal. But, when they start with why, and when their consumers share their beliefs, a sense of belonging occurs and as a consequence, their products symbolise these beliefs.

Simon relates this all back to biology, our craving for a sense of belonging is a basic human instinct.

Biologically speaking, when you look at the brain, Simon points out that his Golden Circle concept directly corresponds to the major levels of the brain.

- The what portion of the Golden Circle takes place in the **neocortex** -where rational thought and analytical thinking occurs.
- The how and why take place in the limbic brain. Where emotions derive and where decisions are made. The limbic brain has no control over language, alas the struggle we face when trying to communicate our feelings sometimes.
- Without the power to put feelings into words, we are forced to rationalise these decisions with any evidence - the what.
- When starting with the what, despite having the facts or evidence, you haven't actually given the power to the decision making limbic brain yet.

- If you engage the limbic brain from the get-go, the how and the why, you go straight to the decision-making part of the brain & allow the decision to be made while the neocortex can rationalise the feeling.

"Companies that fail to communicate a sense of WHY force us to make decisions with only empirical evidence. This is why those decisions take more
time, feel difficult or leave us uncertain."

- The power of the limbic brain can outweigh rational thought. And this is where innovation happens. We take risks that are illogical, driven by emotion. And this is why, we'll pay more money for an Apple MacBook than a PC. Apple products symbolise a user's beliefs, it's a status symbol.

"And that's why the Apple logo is upside down to the user and the right way around for everyone else...

In our individual lives, our missions are inclined to our potentials. Potential is always bigger than the problem. Your potential is infinite and is always bigger than whatever problem you're going through. And your life begins to be okay when you wake up in the morning, and say, *I'm going to walk in the direction of my purpose. I'm going to walk in the direction of my vision.* You're being pulled more by joy. That doesn't mean you're not going to have challenges. We're not praying to have a challenge-free life. We're praying that the challenges that come will activate latent potential. You begin to see, visualize, the kind of life you want to live. Begin to write it down. Begin to dream about it. And then you talk about it. It doesn't mean you talk to everybody, because everyone is not trustworthy. You talk to selected friends. You actually talk to the vision. Talk to the possibility. Talk to love. You talk to peace. You talk to it. And then after a while, you're talking *from* it.

-MICHAEL BERNARD BECKWITH

I think we'd like life to be a train. You get on, pick your destination, and get off when you reach it. But life actually turns out to be a sailboat instead. Every day you have to see where the wind is and check the currents and see if there's anybody else on the boat with you who can help out. The weather changes. The currents change and so does the wind. It's not a train ride, in other words. It's not all about the destination and focusing on not being there yet—though you will be one day, when the train finally pulls into the station.

I have no argument with greatness. But if arriving at my great destination becomes an excuse for dismissing my life now because I haven't found that great purpose yet, that's a waste of a day, if not a life.

BARBARA BROWN TAYLOR

At eleven years old I made a very definitive decision. And my decision was that I wanted to be happy. Above and beyond anything I ever did in my life, I wanted to be happy. But I remember these grown-ups coming to me and saying, "Do you want to be a movie star when you grow up? Do you want to be a dancer? Do you want to be a professional dancer when you grow up? What do you want to be?" And I would say, "Happy." And they would look at me really weird. "No. We said what do you want to be?" And I said, "I want to be happy." That's really all I wanted. Talk about an intention. That's a better intention than a white picket fence.

GOLDIE HAWN

Have you ever seen so many tired people in all of your life? I mean, everybody's tired. Thirty years old and exhausted, twenty-five-year-olds who can't get out of bed in the morning. You know why we're tired? Because we're pretending. It takes so much work to pretend. When you can really be who you are and find out where you fit and function from a place of comfort, then you stop working. You stop wrestling. Absolutely. And when you get in it, that's a life-changing experience. Surrounding yourself with people you want to be like takes you to the next level because they are modelling the lifestyle that you are stepping into, rather than emulating the lifestyle you are stepping away from. Putting yourself in environments with people who are positive or doing what you're doing, whether it's starting a business, owning a company, managing a division—you need to run with people who *have your current and who are in your flow. Do you see that? Do you see that?*

Bishop T. D. JAKES

HOW TO HAVE A MISSION DRIVEN LIFE

1. Identify your purpose: So How Do I Figure Out What My Life-Calling Is?

So glad you asked that question.
Although some prophets may dare, no one can tell you exactly what it is and how it will function. But we can get you pretty close; if you are will enter into a process through which the Lord can make it abundantly clear to you.

Remember, all the prophetic words in the world can't tell you what it is because as scripture tells us, "we see in part and know in part." Besides, someone may see it fairly clearly but often the manner in which they interpret what they see gets distorted, and the filter you hear it through distorts it even further.

I cannot tell you of the number of words that people have given me personally declaring that I "AM going to be filthy rich." One look at my current net worth would tell you those folks were crazy at best and false prophets at worst. In brief, when it comes to prophetic words: chew the meat and spit out the bones.

Psalm 37:4 says, "Delight yourself in the Lord and He will give you the desires of your heart."

It is my expressed belief that God put the desires of your heart in you when you reached planet earth (if not before.) The life-calling you want to discover is already in you. It is His good pleasure to draw it out and He often uses life's circumstances to reveal them to you. (Proverbs 25:2: "It is the glory of God to conceal a thing:

but the honor of kings is to search out a matter.") The problem is that the enemy knew what was in you as well, and has been working overtime to either crush them, or to get you to dismiss them or run from them.

The steps to discovering your life calling are;

- Recover your childhood dreams.
- What you love is a clue to how you were created.
- What you hate is a clue to how you were created.
- What you hear is a clue to how you were created.
- The wisdom you display in certain arenas and life situations is a key to your life-calling/assignment.
- The areas where your creativity is revealed is a clue to your life-calling.
- Personal humility is a major gating factor.
- Describe your tribe; your company of people.
- The enemy usually attacks you at your greatest point of your destiny.
- You will only succeed when your life-calling becomes your obsession.
- A major key to finding your life-calling can be found in your personal history.
- List ten things you think are blocking you from achieving your purpose.
- List fifteen action words you can relate to, or that stir something in you.
- Find out what God is doing, and get in on it.
- If you didn't know how old you were, how old do you think you would be?
- Take all this accumulated data to someone you trust and tell them your story.
- Find Mentors

2. FIND AND START WITH WHY:

The work world is tough: Wake up, go to work, deal with the boss (or if you are the boss, deal with everyone), make money (ideally to make more this year than last year), come home, manage personal life, go to bed, wake up, repeat. That's plenty to deal with every day.

Why get fancy (and waste time) by trying to also understand why you do what you do? The answer to that question isn't fancy; it's simple. Whether you're reading this as an entrepreneur, an employee, as a leader of a team or a division or you want to tackle the WHY of your entire organization, discovering the WHY injects passion into our work.

This is not a formula for success. There are many ways to be successful (by traditional metrics); however, the Golden Circle is a tool to help us achieve long-term, fulfilling success. If you're an entrepreneur, discover your WHY so you can communicate what is singular about your company to your employees and clients or customers.

For example, Apple may not always sell the very best products—ahem, battery life—but if you're someone who wants to "Think Different," you probably swear by Apple on an emotional level you'd never experience with, say, Dell. And knowing your WHY makes it easier to hire the right people. Every entrepreneur wants a staff of true believers, but how can you find those people if you aren't clear on what, beyond hard work, you need them to believe in? If you know your WHY, you can hire people who believe what you believe, which is a much stronger motivator than money. Knowing your WHY is the secret to hiring for "fit."

Knowing your WHY refreshes or renews your passion and connects you to your company's WHY. And should you and that company ever part ways, clearly understanding your own WHY will be an invaluable tool to help choose your next job: a company where you're more likely to "fit," succeed and feel fulfilled.

If you belong to a team or division within an organization, it will likely have its own subculture. In some cases, articulating that team's WHY, the unique contribution the team makes to the organization, can be very powerful. It can help connect those people on the team in a deeper and more meaningful way to the difference the organization makes in the world.

If you want to discover the WHY of the entire organization it will come from one of two sources: The first is from the founder's WHY, which draws from the origin story. If the founder is no longer available, we have a method that engages people in the organization to identify the WHY based on the best elements of the existing culture.

3. ACQUIRE WISDOM, KNOWLEDGE AND UNDERSTANDING:

KNOWLEDGE: *The acquiring of information.*

UNDERSTANDING: *Discerning and valuing important and practical truths.*

WISDOM: *The act of* **applying** *valued truths to any given situation and to life in general.*

Acquiring Wisdom

King Solomon in the Bible placed a great value on acquiring understanding and an even higher value on the application of wisdom. We can be able to live a great simplistic life if we learn to value wisdom like pearls and rubies or hidden treasures.

Here are some of the benefits he promises to those who build their lives on a foundation of wisdom:

A Checking Account of Knowledge. Imagine having a bank account so big that anytime you needed anything, you could simply write a check for it, regardless of the amount. The wise man, Solomon says, stores knowledge in such a "wisdom account." He can draw upon it whenever he encounters any need or any situation that requires a wise decision. Whether he needs a solution in a time of trouble or wisdom to capitalize on an opportunity, he'll always have plenty of knowledge to draw upon. Not so for the foolish. In Proverbs 10:14, Solomon writes, "Wise men store up knowledge, but with the mouth of the foolish, ruin is at hand."

Understanding *Why You Act the Way You Do*. How many times have you done something stupid or out of character and thought, "Why on earth did I do that?" or "What was I thinking?" If you don't understand your behavior, you will repeat it again and again. This is not the case when you acquire wisdom. As Solomon says in Proverbs 14:8, "The wisdom of the prudent is to understand his ways." As you begin to more clearly understand your behavior and natural inclinations, you will begin to make the best choices rather than those to which you're naturally inclined.

A Fountain of Life. From the American history classes Ponce de León was the first European to set foot in Florida. He was searching for the Fountain of Youth. He never found it, because no such fountain exists. Solomon reveals a much more practical and miraculous fountain in Proverbs 16:22. He calls it a "fountain of life." What is it? Understanding. Like a fountain, understanding not only brings life to your deepest needs and desires, it makes you a source of life to those around you as well.

The Favor of Those in Authority. When you were a child, nothing was better than having a coach or a teacher smile at you and pat you on the back and say, "Way to go! Great job!" The same is true for adults. We hate having a person in authority mad at us, whether it is our spouse, our boss, or a police officer. Solomon tells us that when we act wisely, we *will* gain the favor of those in authority (Proverbs 14:35). He also says, "A man shall be commended according to his wisdom" (Proverbs 12:8). A commendation is praise accompanied by an award. In business, that award is usually a bonus or pay increase.

Value and Honor. According to Gary Smalley, the number-one desire of a man is to be admired. And *everyone*—man, woman, boy, and girl—wants to feel valued. And Solomon tells us that the one sure way to be valued and honored is to become wise: "The wise will inherit honor."

Riches. Solomon is talking about both material and spiritual riches. Material riches can be measured in terms of portfolios, bank accounts, and possessions. Spiritual riches are measured by the love, fulfillment, joy, peace, and purpose you experience and the needs of others that you help fulfill. Too many people sacrifice spiritual riches in their pursuit of material riches. I'm convinced that attaining material riches requires much less wisdom than acquiring spiritual ones. Solomon tells us that wise men and women can acquire both. "The crown of the wise," he says, "is their riches" (Proverbs 14:24). Notice he says that riches are the crown, rather than the heart or soul, of the wise. The *heart* of the wise is centered on a value system that reflects true wisdom and the spiritual values and priorities that wisdom brings. That's why the richest man who ever lived could say with authority, "How much better is it to get wisdom than gold! And to get understanding is to be chosen over getting silver."

Protection and Safety. In Proverbs 2:11–12, Solomon writes, "Discretion will protect you, and understanding will guard you. Wisdom will save you from the ways of wicked men, from men whose words are perverse." Wisdom protects us not only from dangerous situations but, equally important, from falling prey to people driven by unethical values, motives, or intentions: the person who wants to con you out of your life savings, or the business associate who wants you to close your eyes to an unethical decision or practice. He's talking about gaining a level of discernment that can see right through the facades of unscrupulous people of all types. Solomon says that this same discernment, understanding, and wisdom will protect a man or woman from those who would seduce them into compromising situations.

Long Life. Those who build their lives on a foundation of wisdom actually live longer. Accept wisdom, Solomon says, and "the years of your life will be many" (Proverbs 4:10). Once again, he distinguishes between knowledge and wisdom. Let me give you another example of the difference. Nearly everyone knows that not wearing seat belts in a car can cost you your life; and yet half of the annual 43,000 fatalities in automobile accidents are people who were not wearing their seat belts. Nearly everyone knows that smoking will shorten your life; yet every year hundreds of thousands of Americans die from diseases caused by smoking. It's not enough to know information. To reap the rewards Solomon promises, you must acquire and consistently exercise wisdom.

4. PLAN DILIGENTLY: DILIGENCE is a learnable skill that combines: *creative persistence,* a *smart-working* effort *rightly planned* and *rightly performed* in a *timely, efficient,* and *effective* manner to attain a result that is *pure* and of the highest quality of *excellence.*

In any endeavor, would you rather pursue it having a strong and unshakable advantage, or having a lasting handicap? King Solomon in the Bible assures us that those who are truly diligent will gain an insurmountable advantage over those who are not.

He says, "The plans of the diligent lead surely to advantage" (Proverbs 21:5). Whether we're competing against companies, individuals, circumstances, or simply time, diligence will give us a unique advantage, one that will result in greater productivity, achievement, wealth, and fulfilment.

In Proverbs 6:6, Solomon tells those who lack diligence to look closely at the ant. The ant "has no commander, no overseer or ruler, yet it stores it provisions in summer and gathers its food at harvest." In other words, the ant is so mission oriented that even without supervision or direction, it does exactly what it needs to do for its benefit and the benefit of the entire colony

When you gain a clear vision of what you want to do, and when you have a **detailed plan** to accomplish that vision, like Solomon's ant, you will take the initiative and gain the diligence to accomplish it. Your mission starts when you are driven to acknowledge the essence of planning effectively to bring your task to a reality.

John Wooden once said " If you fail to plan, you plan to fail. Planning is crucial in every arena of your mission in life. It is what stabilizes your power in you to go forth without complacency. You know, it has to be done. Period. So, you do it.

Plans fail for lack of counsel, but with many advisers they succeed.
—Proverbs 15:22

In any worthwhile endeavor, it's impossible to be diligent without seeking outside counsel and effectively partnering. We all know a little; no one knows a lot. Most of us are deeply knowledgeable in only a few things, and we're totally ignorant and incapable in millions of other things. Yet true diligence demands excellence in every step we take.

The only possible way to achieve excellence in the areas in which we lack the necessary talent or know-how is to seek out counsel and/or effectively partner. When I talk about partnering, I'm referring to asking the help of advisers, counselors, mentors, and anyone else who can provide us with the knowledge and skills we need to achieve excellence in fulfilling our vision.

Throughout the annals of history, no one has achieved any worthwhile goal, significant project, or impossible dream without effectively partnering and seeking outside counsel. If the most successful people in history have needed the help of counselors and partners, why would you think that you can accomplish anything worthwhile without such aid? The fact is, none of us can. The truly diligent do not seek counsel simply when an endeavor is in trouble; rather, they seek counsel from the very beginning, *before* they begin an effort.

This greatly reduces the risk of failure and significantly increases one's probability of success.

5. GET TO WORK:

When God created Adam and Eve, he told Adam to WORK. Say, Work! Work! You see, work was given to man as part of his calling to fulfil, its therefore a gift. A mission driven man never underestimates work. He knows that in all labor there will be profit for him. He assiduously works to bring life to dry bones or natural resources around him in his environment. He is therefore rewarded accordingly.

To live a simple, yet great life – the notion of no work would undermine the unique results we are looking for. Moreover, it will defer the vision and mission creating incompetence and dullness.

Its therefore your duty to embrace work in the field of your calling as it will gradually bring you honor, wisdom and riches.

Now, go out there and do the work.

One Thing You Can Do to fulfil this Chapter of your life.

_____

Listen to your instincts / inner voice to identify your mission in the area of your life or business and go with the flow. It will always lead you to the genuine life filled with purpose and happiness.

_____

PART FOUR:

GREATNESS REIGNS

Chapter 10 – Ignite and share your gifts.

Your gift will make room for you before kings.
—The Bible —

Proverbs 29:18 reads, "Where there is no vision, the people perish." Perishing is the dangerous state of living in a mundane existence without even realizing it. There you are, living your comfortable life, going to the same job—day in and day out—doing the same things. You know your routine so well that you can probably do it without thinking.

There are no dreams or aspirations in front of you, and if you were fired tomorrow, you wouldn't know how to pursue a better life. It would be a sad state of affairs to wake up one morning and realize that you have spent years wandering aimlessly in circles, unclear about your purpose, wasting your gift, and destroying your promise.

What kind of life is that? You can't afford to go another day without a clear direction and focus for your life. I'm not coming at this from a high-and-mighty place. I'm sharing this with you because I've been in that state of perishing, and I had no idea of how to get out until I created a new vision for my life and committed myself to living that new promise.

When I think back to my earlier days, it's painful to remember how much of my life was disconnected from a real vision. I would take any job just to pay the rent. I would date anyone who helped me pass the time.

When I wasn't working, I was hanging out with people who didn't push me any closer to where I needed to be. I was dying slowly, and had I not created a new vision for my life. Perishing is not always about some overdramatic emotional outpour or losing all of your possessions at once. Most often, perishing is a slow, painful process, and if you aren't paying attention, it will trick you into thinking that this is the way things are supposed to be. By failing to have a vision, you are stripping yourself of every possible blessing, relationship, and opportunity. When you sit by and just let your life perish without a vision, it is the most painful kind of death.

ARE YOU IN A STATE OF PERISH?
How do you know if you are perishing or not? Let's get honest about it. You can't expect to create a new life and a new vision for yourself if laziness is part of your routine. Procrastination will not get the job done.

Doing things halfway, improperly, or not at all won't get the job done. Lack of enthusiasm will not get the job done. Unreliability will not get the job done. Being untrustworthy will not get the job done. Any negative trait that derails you from your dreams will not get the job done. Negativity can never be the fuel that drives your gift.

You can also tell if you are perishing if you are the smartest person in your group. If you are the smartest person in the group, you need to get a new group. You cannot be a person who knows it all and can't be told anything, because it will stifle your creativity as well as the creativity of the people around you.

WHAT ARE YOU GOING TO DO WITH YOUR DASH BEFORE YOU DIE?
Another way to put your state of perishing into perspective is to realize that one day your life will come to an end. Whether you want to believe it or not, there will be a casket and a hole in the ground with your name on it. The next home-going service at your church could be yours. And the most important thing on that day won't be the number of flowers that surround your casket or how well the choir sings your favorite hymn.

The only thing that will matter is how well you use that dash between the day you were born and the day you die. I don't want you to spend your days preoccupied with thoughts of death, but I do want you to live your life thinking about how your dash will make a difference in this world. If you've still got breath in your lungs and blood running through your veins, you've got another day to make your dash count. If you're still blessed to wake up and see another day, God has a purpose, a plan, and a destiny for you.

WHEN YOU KNOW THAT YOU KNOW

Nobody but you and God can see it, but you know your gift is in there. It doesn't make sense to most people right now why you're spending so much time on something that looks like a useless hobby, but you know in your heart that it's the key to your future.

At the end of the day, your personal resolve to nurture and grow your gift will be the deciding factor between your success and your failure. I don't care how close you are with your mother or how much your best friend supports your dream; if you don't know and believe in your gift for *yourself*, you will never have the life that God has destined for you.

When you are really living in your gift, you just know it. When you are doing what you are meant to be doing, you can just feel it. When the right opportunity comes along, you won't have to force it. I want you to be able to *live* in a space where your dream is no longer a question of who you are but the answer for everything you are meant to be.

CLIMBING THE MOUNTAIN TO REACH YOUR DREAMS

There is a Scripture in Psalms that says, *"The steps of a good man [or woman] are ordered by the Lord."* I interpreted this Scripture in my life to mean that walking into my destiny is a step-by-step process. I truly believe that God provides all of us with the right steps to get to the right place at the right time. As we continue uncovering how to maximize your gift and finding the best opportunities for using your talents, we're now going to look at how to turn these steps into practical goals for your future.

We all have dreams about the life that we truly want to live. Some people take the leap of faith to walk into their dreams, while others remain on the side-lines waiting for a magical moment to happen. What separates the dreamers from the doers? *Goals.* I don't care how vivid your dreams are: Without goals, your dreams will remain a someday phenomenon instead of today's reality. Goals are the key ingredient that helps us stay focused, consistent, and diligent on our path to achieving our dreams.

THE SUMMIT OF SUCCESS

Another way to think about moving your dreams into goals is to imagine that you are climbing a mountain. Your dream is the summit. Every good mountain climber starts out on his journey with his mind focused on the summit.

Every step forward, every pull of the rope, and even every pause to regain energy is executed by focusing on his goal. Once he reaches the top, he takes a moment to rest, regroup, refuel, and relish in his victory. But every true climber knows that this is just another leg of the bigger journey. Reaching one summit can never be it for the true climber—each time that he pushes his lungs harder, climbs higher, and scales an even more dangerous rock, he knows that it's just preparation for the next journey.

Wherever you are on the mountain—the top, the bottom, midway up, at the rest stop, at the first-aid station, or even poised to stick the flag in the summit—trust and believe that I have been at all those places in my life. I have stuck the flag in the summit. I have been at the rescue station, the first-aid station. I have been halfway up and fallen all the way back down. I have been caught in a cave. I have fallen in between the cracks and crevices of the mountain. I have been trapped on the mountain. I have been covered by an avalanche on the mountain. You name it, on this mountain, I have done it all. I have been told to not even bother climbing because, they said, I didn't have what it takes to make the climb.

I want you to start thinking of your goals as your personal climb to the top of your dream mountain. You can't just expect to wake up tomorrow and become a millionaire, or have your product be a worldwide sensation overnight, or get the position you have been coveting. What goals are you willing to put in place to make your dreams come true? I know that goals can often be overwhelming if you take in the full picture at one time, but think about how you can break down your climb into smaller sections.

You know yourself better than anyone else, so be honest about what will keep you motivated and inspired. Do you need to take this journey with someone else to ensure that you will keep your word? Will it be better to go solo to stay focused? What kind of milestones do you need to keep yourself on track? Are there better times to execute certain parts of your journey than others?

These are good questions to keep in mind as you work your way toward your dream.

Goals are essential because they give you realistic, measurable, and specific targets. They are necessary benchmarks that give you the energy, confidence, and assurance to keep moving in the right direction toward your dream. They can also serve as a handy map for attaining your dreams.

BE A GOALIE!

If step one in your journey to become a small-business owner is to do research with a shop owner whom you admire, then pick up the phone, input the number, and have that conversation. A goal is *not* saying, "Yeah, I've been meaning to talk with Mr. Smith about opening my own shop," and then allowing that statement to fall flat by not following up with some action.

You also have to set up your goals in a way that ensures your success. I know you're excited now that you have this book in your hands and you can really see yourself opening up that bookstore and café you've always dreamed of. But don't sprint out of the gate to apply for that small-business loan or seek angel investors if you don't have a solid business plan in place.

I definitely want you to make big goals, but don't make them so far outside your comfort zone that you set yourself up for failure. If you honestly don't know where to begin, start by just setting up a regular time in your calendar to focus on your dream. If you have an hour to yourself after you drop the kids off at soccer practice, sit down in your favorite spot and make that your goal time.

If there is someone in your church or your community group whom you can recruit for some conversations, allow them to help you chart out your goal process.

Your goals also need to be tailored to your gift, your skill set, and your lifestyle. I don't expect a forty-year-old, married mom of three to work toward her goals at the same pace as a twenty-five-year-old single man.

The woman has an entirely different set of responsibilities that may require more members on her team to help her achieve her goals. By the same token, the twenty-five-year-old man may need more mentors and visionaries to make up for his lack of experience. Create your goals for *you*. Don't waste your energy dwelling on how someone else did what you want to do or how fast they made their goal a reality. Embrace *your* journey and the path God has for *you*.

BELIEVE YOU CAN HAVE IT

God bestowed upon you a gift and placed in you a vision for your gift that does not harm others, because he wants you to have your heart's desire. Do *not* limit your vision because you don't think you are in the right place or know the right people.

The greatest thing about creating your vision is that it is as expansive as your imagination. You deserve a first-class future, and your vision should reflect this belief. Even if you had a past filled with failure, you can create a new vision now. Let go of the past and think toward the future. Leave a history of mistakes behind and dream of wonderful, successful tomorrows.

Success Actions: Write Down Your Vision. Make It Simple and Direct

ASKING FOR WHAT YOU WANT

There are no self-made men. You need others around you for inspiration and motivation. And I'm certain that at some point you will also need them for material resources or advice. Whatever the case, you need to be bold enough to ask. I didn't always feel this way.

In fact, what encouraged me to begin asking was realizing that I had nothing to lose. I also had nothing to prove and nothing to be ashamed of, so rejection was nothing to fear. Recognizing this practically doubled my confidence level.

It strengthened me to go forward and ask. You have no idea of the number of successful people around you who are waiting for someone to come up and ask them for assistance or guidance.

It's okay to sit and brainstorm with like-minded people and share what is going on with you. You may not have to ask for as much as you think. Just the mere fact of your striking up a conversation could be the thing they have been waiting for; maybe this other person is looking for somebody who wants to do something, who is eager to learn, who is eager to share, and that initial conversation will lead to great things. Keep it in perspective; all you need to do is talk to people of like mind, and I promise, they will not mind talking to you.

IDENTIFY WHAT YOU WANT

How do you expect to get what you need if you don't open up your mouth and ask for it? Our lives are a direct reflection of our communication. If you are unwilling to communicate your needs to your employers, customers, partners, and family members, you can't blame them for not giving you what you need. You don't know everything, you don't know everyone, and you can't do it all alone.

ALL POWER, NO SHAME

Various research studies illustrate how powerful it is to ask for what we want. Studies show that in most cases people say yes to those people who ask for what they want far more often than people expect.

Additionally, most requests seem larger in the requester's head than they are to the requestees. Lesson learned? Asking for what you want gives you a better chance of getting it than not asking. So why don't more of us ask for what we want?

A study done by sociologist Annette Lareau showed how kids from different economic backgrounds view asking questions. Kids from affluent and middle-class environments believed that they were entitled to ask for the things they felt they deserved. They almost willed themselves to have what they wanted by creating a habit and value system of asking for what they want.

On the other side, you have people who grew up like me, in an environment where you were viewed as weak if you didn't know something. And don't even get me started about asking for what you need. So often I didn't do that, because I didn't want anyone to know I needed anything. That was the pride that kept me from getting all that I wanted, needed, and actually deserved.

There is no shame in not knowing something, in not having something, or in wanting or needing something. So much of what will determine the difference between a good life and a great life is an ask away. Without shame, you have access to more power.

BUILDING RELATIONSHIPS

While there is power in the ask, there is also risk involved. People may say no. Some may make assumptions based on our wants or needs, and still others may reject us and our boldness in asking for what we want. But the fear of those responses is increased a thousand times when all of our interactions with people are only transactional.

When you interact with people only when you need or want something, they can see your intentions coming a mile away. Asking for what you want becomes a totally different process when you deal with people based on nurtured relationships.

But this can be hard for many of us. We don't want to be vulnerable, and building true relationships requires a higher level of openness. But whether you are attempting to access capital to launch a new business or trying to convince your boss you deserve a raise; a meaningful professional relationship can make all the difference.

When people respond to a request, they are usually not just giving a thumbs-up or a thumbs-down to what you asked for. They are actually assessing what they think of you, the risk involved, and the potential return. How do we begin asking for what we want?

Here are six principles to help you get a yes.

1. KNOW YOUR WORTH. If you don't know your worth, you are allowing someone else to determine it. But knowing your worth is not enough if you don't communicate it boldly. If you have determined you are worth $100,000 a year, you have to be willing to fight to get as close to that value as possible. In fact, you should be prepared to go in asking for more than $100K to give yourself room to negotiate down to what you want.

As with any request, you may not get *exactly* what you want. However, when you know your value and fight for it in a professional way, I guarantee you will walk away from the table with more than if you had asked for nothing.

2. RECOGNIZE WHAT YOU DESERVE. Far too many people—

women in particular—put their wants and needs on the back burner, for the benefit of everyone else. There is nothing noble about denying yourself the life you were destined to have to accommodate someone else. That doesn't mean we don't make compromises for people we love or those we are building businesses with. But if your needs are always being put on hold, you have to pause and reprioritize your values and commitments. Warning: Be careful that you don't confuse what you deserve, which is what you work for, with a sense of entitlement, which is what you want but didn't work for.

3. GET SPECIFIC. It is important to be specific about what you want and need. Failure to communicate what you need will add frustration and increase your timeline to gaining your success.

4. DON'T ASSUME ANYTHING. People are not mind readers. I don't care how well you know someone: Never assume that they know what you want or need. Even if you think they "should" know, get crystal clear about your needs beforehand.

5. COMMUNICATE YOUR VALUES. Be firm about what you will and will not stand for. The quickest route to frustration is a failure to communicate your value system. This can be challenging when you are in a place of real need. But don't be someone who can be easily bought. Don't compromise your standards.

6. RECOGNIZE THAT "NO" IS NOT A REJECTION. The bank, your boss, and even your significant other will not always say yes. They may not be able to give you what you want. Do the best you can to see the situation from all sides and not just your own before you cut off a relationship, turn down an opportunity, or burn a bridge.

Your gift is waiting for you to fight for what you want. When you build a world that looks the way you want it to, you are giving your gift more room to grow. You have come too far now to talk a good game about what you want without asking for what you want. The worst thing that can happen is someone will say no.

The best thing that can happen when you ask for what you want is . . . You Get What You Want and Need.

DIVERSIFYING YOUR GIFTS

You are not a sell out if you expand your gifts and talents for wider appeal among a broader audience or a bigger arena. The more open you are, the faster you will realize your dreams. An expansive vision is necessary when reaching for your life's possibilities. We cannot allow small-mindedness to interfere with our rewards.

Step outside your comfort zone and try something new, something adventuresome, when utilizing your gift. The Bible says, "I've come that they may have life, and have it abundantly." Nowhere in that Scripture does it say, "I've come that you might have a comfortable, safe, boxed-in life that makes everybody happy."

Diversifying your gift presents you with the opportunity to reach people whom you wouldn't have been able to connect with previously. There are windows of blessings that God has just for you if you have the faith to take your gift to the next level.

Writing this book is a way of diversifying my gift. We have to learn to dream bigger than our past and current circumstances to create a bigger picture that will inspire us to move forward.

SHARE YOUR GIFTS

Sharing your gifts is an act of creating abundance for others through the act of rendering your whole abilities, talents and crafted creativities. Everyone on this planet has a gift. A gift that pulls him or her with ease on whatever he or she does. Most scenarios give us a vivid scene where one works and seems never to get tired. Your gift is mostly your passion or what you love to do. It will never seem like work to you. The world is gradually filled with amazing things because of the outpour of gifts from various individuals of different countries. When you begin to share your gift, it begins to serve as a solution to a problem of someone else which can later lead to profit or non-profit according to how you use it.

If you haven't found your gift yet, Keep looking and don't stop until you find it. Your gift is normally an ability which you find its adaptability and usage easier before many. The many recognizes it as a hard task whiles you see it in a light of ease.

Sharing your gifts will make the world fall in love with you and most times will create an avalanche of abundance for you, your family and everyone around you. So, what are you waiting for?

A gift can be in a trillion variety of fields uniquely given to every man on earth. A man who finds his gift early, embraces it and put on a cloak of a choice of improving or taking it to a higher level would be rewarded in all sorts of ways. It will therefore lead him to his riches earlier or lately depending on when he identified it and took an irrefutable action to provide value for someone else with it. We can see people of such analogies who did that – Bill Gates, Warren Buffet, Elon Musk, Jeff Bezos and others which you might know whose gifts solved huge problems in the world. They all had an early start with a gift in computing which sprout a seed from infancy whiles holding on to it. I have come to realize that parenting can also play a factor for a child to realize his or her inborn gifts – the mother or father helps directs him or her to that path when on a consistent basis, they realize that the child is doing excessively well in a particular field or strongly attached to a way of doing things. That can bring an aha! moment.

Begin to ask yourself " what is it that I can be than can distinct myself from others?" – This question can throw an answer into a form of launching a business idea, helping people in a unique way, singing in a grand pitch, being an investor, Doing hair, etc.

I can't name them all because there are billions of gifts in the world distributed by the Maker. If anyone tells me that " Well, I don't think I have any gift. My response will be; You have been carrying it all this while but you haven't made any effort to identify, embrace it and carry on with a choice of working hard on it to become obsessed in mastering it." That's it. No B.S.

You can be thankful for your gifts but you cannot be proud of your gifts. Because your gift was given to you but you can be proud of your choices by working hard on your gifts to take it to another level on mastering it. Your gift is like a seed, it has to be watered and nurtured so that it can grow into a giant tree with fruits. I believe you are going to change the world with your gift and your choice behind it is going to make it come into reality. If you are with me, Say; Yes!

It's time to explore your gift like never before. The world needs your gift, whatever you carry, we need it and when you avail yourself by bringing it forth – we will reward you. Says' 'the world".

One Thing You Can Do to fulfil this Chapter of your life.

---

*Leverage your **gifts** in many ways which would ultimately lead you to future freedom and independence creating a simple, yet great life for you.*

Chapter 11 – Take it to the Next Level

Surround yourself with gallant size people.

Oprah Winfrey.

Fox: Checkmate! – Ugh! Who is your buddy? Well, my buddy, it's not just a buddy because there are more buddies of mine.

Scott: What! How many?

Fox: Well, about 1000. But the unfortunate thing is that they are all just like me.

Scott: You! Oh! Such a pity. Why on earth am I even sitting here with you?

Fox: Hey. What's wrong?

Scott: I think you are missing a valuable lesson in life.

Fox: What's that?

Scott: You damn fool, your friends defines who you are. I now understand the reason for your awful nature.

This is it, taking it to the next level – What am I taking it to the next level? – Your gift. As I said before, everyone on this earth has a unique gift and you carry one. Why am I obsessed with your gift, because I believe however you think you are beginning to create advancements whether you are in the initial phase or in its freefall, you still need to sharpen it to mastery and excellence? Guess what, there is one thing, that if you do, would bring that to a glorious peak.

And what is that? Drum roll!

The people that you surround yourself with. In this dimensional power of simplifying your life. It will come to its radiance of understanding when you begin to tickle the effects of what the people who serve as your closest friends, business associates, trustworthy personnel's etc who are in your inner or mastermind circle defines you critically.

Well, you might have heard this before, and how does it got to do with simplifying your life. Now, every group has their type of beliefs, values, cultures or simply way of life they adhere to. If your group strips you by not challenging or stretching you to advance in your gifts, it would ultimately climax the downfall of your potential.

Now begin to look around for the people who surrounds you every day of your life whom you consciously or unconsciously invited them into your life. They are either gallant or chickens. Either they are helping you to grow your potential or they are sucking or draining life out of you every time you are in their midst.

So, let's do this small exercise. Begin eliminating people in your circle who are not helping you in any way or pushing you to think and function as a human being them and do that with a flexibly with a plan and thinking ahead. Now, its gonna get rough in the way. Gently do it.

When that is done, the remaining friends or associates would definitely become the people who are like-minded. They are the people who understands the simple ways of nature, implemented them and living it. Not only are you going to draw others like you in your realm but it will significantly increase your being to a higher level.

The power of relationships has a gross effect on you as a social being. You either conform to the ways of others or they conform to your ways. You choose. Life on this earth is so short to be cutting angles with the wrong people. Now, the strong thing that I believe would work to a substantial effect is the notion of moving to the future and imagine if the very sphere of people you are with currently would satisfy you in that age, Let's say 80. Are you going to hang around with those life draining individuals? No!

There is an interesting dialogue which happened between an artist and a nearby passers-by.

This is a story of a man named Lexonart- a pro artist - who found this man nearby. The name of the man in this photo is Adrian. I met him whilst driving home from work on a sunny Thursday afternoon in 2017. Upon meeting him our conversation was brief but humorous and fruitful. He was walking along a roadway with a bottle of Pepsi mixed with alcohol in his hand and a slight stagger. I slowed down to check if he was okay and as he turned and looked in the car with a faint disoriented smile, an image of a clock and mask hit me. I immediately pulled over because I knew something was building imaginatively.

I asked him if he was okay to which he nodded gleefully. I expressed to him what I do and how seeing his face had inspired me, to which he responded in our Jamaican dialect, "Yuh a funny man? Why mi face haffi inspire yuh?"

In English terminology his response translates as,

"Are you gay? Why did my face inspire you?" This was spoken in jest.

I chuckled and said, "No, I'm an artist, and technically I didn't admire your face, it just gave me an idea."

We both had a good laugh and a fruitful conversation ensued.

I expressed the idea to him and he became thrilled to be a part of it with the condition that I mirror an aspect of his life story in the shoot, pay him and buy him a drink of rum. I showed up the next day but without the rum and we ran into a little problem, he was unfocused and seemed troubled. After trying to shoot for the first couple minutes nothing came to fruition.

I asked him what was wrong and he expressed that he needed a drink to be steady, get the edge off.

I told him I couldn't do that because it goes contrary to my art and why I create.

"I cannot give you something that would harm you so I can help others."

He then responded by saying, "This one bottle will HELP more people than it will harm me. I will sober up, if not, I will buy it myself with the money you'll give me." A bit of laughter erupted amongst us but eventually I conceded as he was quite an intellectual man.

This was his story.
He died the following year in 2018.
His death wasn't alcohol related but his message was that LIFE is a leaf that's falling from the branch of a low hanging tree. Live fully before it hits the ground because time cannot be harnessed.

What is the lesson of the story – If there is anything you have to do on this earth which you have, you better do it Early because the CLOCK IS TICKING every moment.

I can tell you the richest place on the planet – Guess what! It is the **Cemetery.** It is where ideas which were not given life, projects which were halted, books unwritten, talents untapped, abilities misused, AND lives not lived fully.

Now, go out there and take your gift to the next level through ultimate Service fuelled with passion.

Chapter 12 – Service Equals Greatness

---

*If you want to be great-SERVE -**Jesus***

Keep away from those who try to belittle your ambitions. Small people always do that, but the really great make you believe that you too can become great - Mark Twain

Greatness is the seed of life deposited in every human spirit at creation. Just as the breath of life was blown into mankind to become a living soul, so was this gift put in you. Greatness is the evidence of God's DNA in humanity. It is one thing acknowledging there is greatness residing in you but it is a whole different ballgame to bring it to bare, through its activation.

Service to mankind is undoubtedly the hallmark to greatness. The question is how come everyone is not living up to their greatness? This is the quandary most people face in life—some even go to the extent of saying, "If we all become great, who would serve us?"

Greatness is not achieved through studies in higher education. It is also not associated with the number of people you control and supervise. It is not social affluence or political influence and charisma. Neither is it liken to the accumulation of wealth nor the ability to reach the summit of fame or power.

The myth and optical illusion of stardom have hoodwinked this generation into thinking that greatness always has something to do with fame, power, wealth, intellectualism etc. Hence, we oftentimes look for quick ways to achieve prominence, which has brought about pain, misery, greed, and social degradation upon this generation. Greatness is the sacrifice and service rendered to humanity regardless of the threat of freedom and social ostracism which is sometimes affiliated with it.

The great people we revere, and read about today were not necessarily the aristocrats or celebrities of their days, but servants to worthy causes in their communities and nations in their era. In most cases, they were either public enemies or outlawed. Their passion to leave the world a better place than they met it, often motivated them to sacrifice their personal freedom for a greater cause.

Some toppled kingdoms, others pushed for justice and equal rights, some wrestled with lions and went through fire, others were martyred, some turned disadvantage situations to advantage, won battles, and routed foreign armies.

Greatness has always been akin to sacrifice, discomfort, selflessness, or loneliness. Besides, no great person sets off to achieve greatness. It is in the persistent service and sacrifice to a cause greater than ourselves that elevates them to the pinnacle of life.

Once upon a time, in the shadow of a mountain, a herd of sheep lived and grazed on the cool, green grass. As the herd grazed close to a tall oak tree, there lay a small copper-colored lump of fur. The ewe bent down sniffing carefully but the lump did not move. The ewe tried prodding the lump with its nose but it wouldn't move.

The ewe could see its small chest rise with each breath, so it decided to lie down beside it to give it warmth and see if it would wake up. At dusk, the small furry bundle began to stir. The ewe licked its face and it nuzzled closer finding warm milk to drink.

As time went by, the ewe continued to take care of the foundling as part of the herd. All the sheep noticed a disparity between them and this animal. The animal was taller than the biggest ram and its' coat was the color of the warm, summer sunset rather than the clouds.

Its copper-colored face was broader and her mouth was filled with big, sharp teeth. But it mingled with the herd going up the mountain paths, drank out of the streams and nibbled the grasses like all good sheep.

This small copper-colored lump of fur was a cub of a lion living life among sheep! They all lived together in the meadow eating, sleeping and moving as a heard. Soon this "Lion-sheep" became clever in spotting dangerous animals, so it guarded the herd at night and moved in front of the herd during the day.

One day, the herd went to the stream to drink water where they had set their eyes on a dangerous animal lurking for their prey. Just as they all put their mouth in the river and the "Lion-sheep" saw its reflection in the water, then it jumped and ran off with the herd out of fear of seeing a dangerous lion not recognizing it was its own image.

On another occasion out in the meadow, a sound rang out and the herd ran together for safety; this time again, the "Lion-sheep" ran off initially but stopped and turned towards the noise. Around the tree came the largest beast they had ever seen. The herd bunched closer with the cub in front as it moved toward the strange beast.

The ewe bleated out to warn the "Lion-sheep" but it kept going, looking at the beast unafraid and stopping just inches away. The beast saw itself in the other and nodding its head went to the stream. The "Lion-sheep" followed. As both animals bent down to drink, the "Lion-sheep" saw its own reflection again and looking over saw the face of the strange beast in the still water.

The images looked alike. Shocked, the "Lion-sheep" drew back from the edge of the water and toward the herd, but the big beast stepped into its path, blocking the "Lion-sheep's" way roaring at it.

The "Lion-sheep" roared back and as the other sheep backed further away in fear, terrified with the noise the strange lion communicated to the "Lion-sheep," "Don't run away from who you are. You may have grown up here with a herd of sheep, but you have greatness within you. You are strong, independent and brave. There are many more things that you can do, places you can go and other animals more to see than the sheep and this safe, green meadow. Come with me".

This strange lion was challenging and stirring the greatness in the "Lion-sheep. "The "Lion-sheep" had always believed it was different from the sheep despite growing up with them and cosying in the comfort of the meadow. It fancied moving about the mountain but longed to see higher, go farther and do adventurous activities.

For the first time, the "Lion-sheep" could see its true self mirrored in the eyes of the lion. Now, the "Lion-sheep" understands that it is not weird as it thought but rather it's part of the traits of its family of greatness that it has not yet discovered.

The "Lion-sheep" had a choice to stay with the safety of the herd, living in fear and at the mercy of the other beast or to respond to the burning desire to discover its true self although challenging, unfamiliar, and audacious. The "Lion-sheep" resolved to step out of its comfort zone and activate the greatness residing latent within it.

Similarly, most people are born with greatness to change our world to become a better place but because of their association, their seed of greatness is largely untapped. German philosopher, Arthur Schopenhauer said, "Great minds are like eagles, and build their nest in some lofty solitude." In other words, great people face and address challenges in life, see far beyond and do things differently than the great masses.

The following are signs that take place privately when your greatness is being activated:

• **Misfit among your association**— when the seed of greatness within you starts to evolve, you will feel like a lion amid sheep. In other words, you will be unconventional in your declarations, values, and philosophy of life.

Things that were irrelevant to you before, suddenly becomes significant. This is the time when friends and people around you are likely to scorn the emerging person within you. I would advise you not to disclose your dreams to just any person you meet at this stage, since you could also be distracted, discouraged, or derailed during this period of transition.

• **See yourself as you should be**—most people consciously or subliminally try to avoid this experience because it exposes the lapses, failures, and how far they are lagging behind in their purpose in life. In other words, here, your life becomes like a timeline in a movie and you see where you are presently vis-à-vis where you should have been in life.

The quandary here is that most people tend to surrender when they see they lag far behind in their purpose or dream in life, instead of using this sentiment as an impellent to simulate their purpose. Comer Cantrell said, "Sometimes the greatest inspiration is born out of desperation." I concur with American professional basketball player for the Sacramento Kings, Isaiah Thomas who said, "No matter how many shots you miss, always believe you're going to make the next one."

• **Feel energized around greatness**—Greatness attracts greatness. One of the signs of the activation of the greatness in you is that the attitude, values, and accomplishments of great people generate a strong desire to believe in your ability to achieve your own dream. That is to say, the life of great people becomes a touchstone and a motivation for you in your quest to get to greatness yourself.

• **Internal restlessness to act**—this is the most complicated and frustrating part of the experience. Most times when you know what you are supposed to do or where you should be in life and owing to reasons beyond human comprehension, you are not on that level, you begin to experience internal turmoil. When you envisage the gap between where you are and where you are going, it makes you fretful; especially when you have not yet begun the journey.

The most difficult thing is not the discovery of your purpose or the articulation of your vision but the process, i.e. the distance between where you are and your destination in life.

Greatness has largely been misconstrued by society today so much that it has now been associated with power, social charisma, and fame; an average person today is determined to be famous, wealthy, or powerful regardless of the means to get there. Service and sacrifice are no more the symbol of greatness but rather charisma and reputation. It is no longer significance but success.

Richard W. Shelly, Jr. cautioned that "A desire for bigness has hurt many folks. Putting oneself in the limelight at the expense of others is a wrong idea of greatness. The secret of greatness rather than bigness is to acclimate oneself to one's place of service and be true to one's own convictions. A life of this kind of service will forever remain the measure of one's true greatness."

As you set off on the journey of greatness, remember, "You are not here merely to make a living. You are here in order to enable the world to live more amply, with greater vision, with a finer spirit of hope and achievement. You are here to enrich the world, and you impoverish yourself if you forget the errand," Woodrow Wilson.

On Sunday 2/4/2018, the Super Bowl LII was played. For the first time, I watched an entire Super Bowl game, not just the halftime performance as was my custom. I was cheering for the underdogs, the eagles, and they won!

My most memorable moment of the event wasn't the half-time performance. It was when Ram Trucks used a talk by Dr. Martin Luther King Jr. in a commercial.

On February 4, 1968, Dr. King said the following, which Ram Trucks used as the voice over for their commercial:

*"If you want to be important — wonderful. If you want to be recognized —wonderful. If you want to be great — wonderful. But recognize that **he who is greatest among you shall be your servant. That's a new definition of greatness.** By giving that definition of greatness, it means*

that everybody can be great, because everybody can serve. You don't have to have a college degree to serve. You don't have to make your subject and your verb agree to serve. You don't have to know about Plato and Aristotle to serve. You don't have to know Einstein's theory of relativity to serve. You don't have to know the second theory of thermodynamics in physics to serve. You only need a heart full of grace, a soul generated by love. And you can be that servant." Martin Luther King, Jr

Dr. King wasn't the original author of the idea of greatness defined in terms of service to humankind. He as quoting another freedom fighter, another transformational leader who had lived over two thousand years before Dr. King. He was expounding on a life principle that Jesus of Nazareth taught his disciples.

One day, two of Jesus' disciples, James and John, the sons of Zebedee, came to him and as "Teacher," they said, "we want you to do for us whatever we ask.

"What do you want me to do for you?" he asked. They replied, "Let one of us sit at your right and the other at your left in your glory."

These two disciples of Jesus were asking him to make them great. In essence to give them greatness.

Jesus proceeded to gently reply to them:

"You don't know what you are asking. Can you drink the cup I drink or be baptized with the baptism I am baptized with?"

"We can," they replied, without missing a beat.

Jesus said to them, "You will drink the cup I drink and be baptized with the baptism I am baptized with, but to sit at my right or left is not for me to grant. These places belong to those for whom they have been prepared."

When the other ten of Jesus' disciples heard that about what had happened and became indignant with James and John, that's when Jesus called them together and taught them what Dr. King called a new definition of greatness.

Jesus called all his twelve disciples together and told them, "You know that those who are regarded as rulers of the Gentiles lord it over them, and their high officials exercise authority over them. Not so with you. **Instead, whoever wants to become great among you must be your servant, and whoever wants to be first must be slave of all.** For even the Son of Man did not come to be served, but to serve, and to give his life as a ransom for many."

That is where Dr. King got his amazing definition of greatness.

Service equals greatness.

CONCLUSION

I am grateful, you took your time in this time and moment in space to bring these ideas into your mental and heart faculties. You must connect ideas to ideals and excitement to action. You must do more with this book than place it on a shelf or file it away in your electronic reading device. Don't get me wrong. I love being able to share my ideas here with you in these pages.

Reading is the gymnasium of the mind. It is the place where thoughts are exercised and minds are stretched and challenged.

However, through tranquillity and deep reflection we are able to search the heart for answers that the mind alone doesn't contain. The mind may guide you in what to do, but the heart affirms your passion to do it. This is what will ultimately move you to motion.

Somewhere in your passions lie the clues to your deeper purpose. It is my hope that you will recognize the divine investment placed within you and garner all your resources to steward this treasure for the future before you. In short, you have what it takes! All that you need is within you and can be accessed instinctively.

Understanding this truth secretes confidence, which I'm convinced has a lot to do with overcoming obstacles and releasing your inherent, resilient power. This is not just a book that you've just read. I believe with the garner of resources, ideas, wisdom and knowledge you got from this book; it is going create a new dimension of vortex of simple abundance in your life. In this world, the greatest thing that would resonate with you at the core of your being is when someone tells you- *Hey! Do you know what? You have changed my life.* Really! *Yes - Simple, yet Great* will continue to change billions of lives as it has changed you in a new reality. I would encourage you to fasten your seatbelt as you begin your ride in a new phase of higher awakening and awareness. Remember, Life is meant to be joyful and exhilarating on this earth. If yours is currently otherwise, upon reading this book, get ready for a new journey of;

- *Sparking of life changing ideas*
- *Living a true life*
- *Being yourself*

- *Launching your dream businesses*
- *Travelling the world*
- *Living a simple, yet rich and great life.*
- *Being on top of the world.*
- *Being wiser.*
- *Acknowledging the treasures of wisdom and knowledge and understanding.*
- *Being humbler. Etc*

Now GO out there and do your very best – Your time on this earth is limited, so don't waste it living someone else's' life.

Thank you. I love you with all my heart. Remember, We're always ONE.

ACKNOWLEDGEMENTS

Great artistry works always come from merging of powerful minds. I want to use this space to thank the contributing members of this book whose efforts and words brought it to life.

I am profoundly in awe with Jephthah – my long-time friend, who had my back when the whole world was crashing against me.

I thank you Anita Boabeng for checking on me periodically to get a hold of the manuscript to perfect it.

I am grateful to Patience Dwamena for her ideas behind the cover and content of the book.

Oh, I am indebted in gratitude to the profound thinkers, movers and shakers in this world whose life has impacted mine leading me to impact others like a chain of chemical reaction through this book.

I thank Mr. Elder Bright Appiah for his guiding principles and embracing this book at first sight. I am grateful to you, Mrs. Joana Appiah for a heartfelt connection to this book on a deeper level.

Finally, I Wanna thank you mum for seeing me through my darkest periods in my life. You will always be on our hearts even though you are weird sometimes.

To all, my readers globally – I am so much happy and I promise to continue the message of releasing ground-breaking ideas, experiences and thoughts throughout the world through every node of mine as long as I live.

ABOUT THE AUTHOR

Emmanuel Dwamena is an author, an online publisher, a computer scientist, a tech savvy (Youtuber and Internet marketer), researcher and an emerging thinker. He is the founder of the upgrowing YouTube Channel called **Leading Posts** which serves to inform humanity on a grand scale.

He loves to write novels and non-fiction books especially on Technology, Business, Finance, Self-development, Productivity and Leadership and life experiences. *He believes he has a mission to render unto humanity. To fulfil the highest, truest expression of himself as a human being. To fulfil the promise that the creator dream when he dreamt of the cells that made him.*

He has purposed and aspires to serve God and man *with mastery and excellence*, to create a chain of businesses that will improve or evolve humanity by solving daunting problems using technology, knowledge, wisdom and imagination, moreover, providing support to people from many angles.

He currently teaches the teens in his Church to awaken and grow in spirituality so that they can find their stay on this earth joyful and experience a life of bliss.

BIBLIOGRAPHY/ REFERENCES

1. Dying to be Me – **Anita Morjani**
2. Find your Why – **Simon Sinek**
3. Discovering your Purpose – **Dr. Myles Munroe.**
4. My personal Best – **John Wooden**
5. Leadership by **John Wooden**
6. Finding your life's calling – **Jim Banks**
7. How to be A Bawse – A guide for conquering life – **Lily Singh**
8. Mastery – **Robert Greene**
9. Round the World – **Andrew Carnegie**
10. The Hidden DNA of the Four Companies, Amazon, Google, Apple, and Facebook – **Fox Scott**
11. The Everything Store – **Brad Stone.**
12. Act like a Success – **Steve Harvey**
13. Discovering your path and life's purpose – **Oprah Winfrey**
14. The Richest Man Who Ever Lived – **Steven Scott**
15. Simple Living – **www.Wikipedia.com**
16. Instinct – The Power to unleash your inner drive -**Bishop T.D Jakes**

This Page is intentionally left blank.

NOTES

www.ingramcontent.com/pod-product-compliance
Lightning Source LLC
Chambersburg PA
CBHW070350300526
45791CB00025B/1800